Job Interview

An Essential Guide Containing 100 Common Questions, Winning Answers and Costly Mistakes to Avoid

Contents

Part 1: Job Interview

Prepare to Get Hired: Top 100 Common Questions and Winning Answers

Introduction

The chances are that you are looking to get a new job. Maybe you are hoping to get your dream job. You could be looking to get your first job. It could even be that you have decided to make a career change. No matter your reason, you have come to the right place. Acing the interview is the first step in making sure you get the job you want.

Lucky for you, interviewing is a skill that anybody can easily master. Superior intellect or physical strength is not needed. A game plan and little bit of practice are all you need. This book will provide you with everything you need to know to create that game plan. The key to acing an interview is knowing how to answer the questions properly.

Most job interviews will fall into three categories. Nearly 70 percent of interviews are disappointing. People go in unprepared and struggle through all of the questions, providing answers that are vague or don't even answer the question.

The next 20 percent are fairly decent interviews. People make sure they are prepared, and they provide relevant and clear answers.

The last ten percent is the best of the best. They can answer the questions with confidence. They make the interview fun and the interviewer's job easier. These people will be able to get any job that they want.

The goal of this book is to help you become that third group. The best candidates aren't necessarily the most gifted. They don't have some secret formula for having an amazing interview. Their key to success is being prepared. They research and find out what questions are most often asked and they get ready to answer those questions.

Business students will often be very good at the interview process because they learn what questions are most often asked and the best way to answer them. They also practice with others. Basically, they rehearse for their interview.

Unfortunately, there are many other students and people who don't get this type of preparation. It is crazy to think that this isn't a part of the college curriculum considering all of those students are going to want to get a job once they graduate. They may be ready for the job, but they aren't ready to prove they are worth the time and money.

We will look at eleven different categories of questions that are most often asked during interviews. This also includes the "Do you have any questions?" This is likely the hardest part of the interview process. You will have to customize your answers according to your experience, but the answers provided in this book will help to aim you in the best direction.

Imagine how great you will feel when you leave your interview knowing that you aced it. If you follow the tips in this book, you *will* get to experience that sensation.

The skill will also be helpful in other areas of your life so that you can be more persuasive. Interview skills can help you with not only landing a job but also in persuading other people. That means this book can be helpful even if you aren't planning on finding a new job.

Before we get into the questions, let's take a look at a few steps you can take to make sure you are fully prepared for your interview.

First, it is important that you do some research on the type of job. A simple Google search will provide you with thousands of sample descriptions. From there, you can write down the main responsibilities that the job will require. This helps you to get ready for the questions and will help to set you apart from other people applying for the job. After you have figured out what your employer is looking for, you will be able to prepare the best answers.

Next, research some job-specific details. If you can, find a description of the specific job that you are looking to get. Employers will sometimes post job descriptions for their open positions online. If you aren't able to find one, contact a person at the company and ask for one. Most of the time HR or hiring managers will happily provide you with a job description.

Read through the description and write out some notes about what they expect. This will provide you with a cheat sheet for creating your answers. This is much like getting the answers for a test before you have to take it. Employers will typically let you know exactly what they want from you. Make sure you frame your answers so that they highlight your skills with the needed responsibilities.

Next, get ready for the different types of questions. The majority of the interview questions will fall into six main groups. There are different variations, which we will go into, but preparing for these six categories are typical:

1. Opening – These questions will normally involve your background, work experience, and education.

2. Interest – These ask about what your interests are.

3. Fit – These questions help the interviewer figure out if you are a good fit for their position. These are sometimes referred to as behavior questions because they may sometimes ask you how you would act in a certain situation.

4. Case – These are made to test your thinking skills.

5. Odd-Ball – These are questions to see how well you can think on your feet.

6. Closing – These are used to get any last bits of information that the interviewer may need to make their decision.

This book, however, has been broken down into eleven types of questions. This is because some of the above categories can be broken down further to help you prepare more for the interview. We will cover:

1. Personal questions

2. Questions about your experience

3. Questions about your strengths and weaknesses

4. Questions about the position and company

5. Questions about the future

6. Questions to see how you handle stress

7. Questions about you to expect from the company

8. Questions about your last job

9. Questions to find out why you want the job

10. Questions on why should they hire you

11. Do you have any questions?

Dos and Don'ts

Let's go over some quick things you need to make sure that you keep in mind.

- Be grateful – The interviewer is using their time to speak with you. Make sure you tell them that you appreciate it. Start the interview with a "Thank you" and end the interview with a "Thank you." Follow up after the interview with a "Thank you."

- Be truthful – All of your responses should be truthful. It is the right thing, plus the interviewer will fact-check everything you say. If you lie, and they catch you, you can kiss your chances of working with them goodbye.

- Frame your answers – You are going to learn how to frame your answers throughout this book so that you don't end up rambling or being vague.

- Provide examples – Facts are great, but if you can provide stories of when you have faced certain situations, that is even better. People will remember these stories. Make sure they are brief, though, but also with enough detail so the interviewer can picture it.

- Be concise – You want to make sure your answers are long enough to provide enough information but short enough so that you don't control the conversation.

- Be specific – Employers are listening to hear specifics about the things you have accomplished.

- Be passionate – Employers are looking for people who will actually like doing their job. Show them that you like the work you are applying to do.

- Be positive – You need to focus on the positive parts of your experiences. Employers are looking for those who can remain positive in all circumstances.

- Don't be wordy – Don't start droning on and on. As you practice, figure out how you can be brief but thorough in your answers.

- Don't be negative – No matter how rough you have had it, or how mean your bosses have been, don't talk about these things in your interview.

- Don't be personal – Don't bring up politics, religion, hobbies, friends, family, or anything unrelated to the job. Plus, it is illegal for them to ask you questions about family and age.

- Don't be modest – You shouldn't be humble while in an interview. You want them to be impressed by what you can do and have done. Share awards you have received that have to do with the job. They want to hear about your accomplishments.

- Keep your answers limited to about two minutes or less. You want them to be long enough to grab the attention of the interviewer and not so long as to control the conversation.

- Keep your passion related to the position you are applying for.

- Briefly talk about your work experience. You should be able to do this in four to eight sentences. Later on, you will be able to go into more detail.

- Talk about promotions. They like to hear when you have earned levels of increasing responsibility.

- Do make sure that your interviewer knows you are interested in the role. Tell them explicitly what it is that you want from the job and why their position is going to provide you with that.

- Make sure you are crystal clear on your career goals. If you aren't sure what your career goals are, figure them out before you get started with your interview.

- Take a look back at the jobs you have had and take notes of what you have liked about each of them. Then let the interviewer know how their position is going to help you build on these experiences.

- Create a 30-60-90-day plan before you go into the interview. Make sure you have a copy of your plan with you in case you are given a chance to share it. This will show that you are excited and proactive about your job.

- Make sure you have realistic goals. Interviewers want candidates who want to grow in their careers, but they want somebody who is also realistic about the time it takes to do this. Show them that you are interested in and progressing at a reasonable pace.

- Talk about the things that you do outside of work that helps to improve your skills. Interviewers love people who love their job so much that they spend their spare time improving their abilities.

- If you don't get asked a question that would allow you to share your 30-60-90-day plan, then don't push it on them. You don't want to come off pushy. The interviewer gets to control the conversation, not you.

Keep in mind that interviewers love to speak with candidates who show that they are passionate about the work they have to offer. You have to make sure that your answers reflect this passion. This can be shown through your research and the fact that you believe the company and position is a good fit for you.

You should now be ready to ace your interview!

Talking About Yourself

These are the questions that interviewers ask to get to know you. This gives them a good understanding as to who you are and the type of person you are. Most of these questions won't be directly related to the job that you are applying for. These questions give the interviewer insight into your personality.

Sometimes these questions will confuse the interviewee because they don't seem important for the job. While they may seem unimportant, they aren't. The more prepared you are for them, the better off you will be. If you bomb these questions, it might not kill your interview, but it will make you stand out in a *bad* way.

Let's take a look at some specific questions that you could be asked.

Tell Me about Yourself

This is probably the most common question you will hear during an interview. This is also normally the very first question. The interviewer is looking to understand your communication skills, experiences, and interests. How you answer this question is going to set the tone for the remainder of the interview. If you can impress them with your answer, you will put yourself at the top of their list, and they will be rooting for you.

If you don't do well on this, it is going to be extremely hard for you to recover. The interviewer may even mentally eliminate you from the running, and they will try to find every reinforcement for this belief that they can.

However, this is the easiest question to prepare for. Since you have spent some time researching the position you are applying for, you should know exactly what they want to hear. Make sure that your answer highlights the interests you have that fall in line with the position.

You don't want to end up falling into the trap of talking about your personal interests. They don't care if you are learning to play the piano or to knit—unless that directly relates to the position you are applying for. They are interested in hearing why they should hire you. After you have been hired, then maybe they may take an interest in your interests, but until that time comes, focus on the attributes that make you look good for the job.

Make sure you summarize your relevant work experience at this point, and you should let them know what position you are looking for. Naturally, this desired role would need to be the one in which you are applying for.

We are going to take a look at a great way to answer this question if applying for the position of a marketing assistant. This job may require you to identify campaign ideas, manage different project teams, and write agency briefs:

> *"I enjoy looking for creative solutions to problems. While in college, I was part of the yearbook staff. This is where I led a project to make the first online version of the college's yearbook. During a summer internship, I created social media sites for three organizations. Once I graduated from North Eastern University with my Bachelor's Degree in Marketing, I started work at 'Too Cool for You Marketing Agency' where I created campaigns for clients, managed project teams, planned projects, and wrote project briefs. I have been with them for three years. During this time, I have moved from Assistant Manager to Associate Manager. I was*

also presented with the Most Creative Marketing Campaign Award. I want to move into a role where I can have more responsibility in marketing decisions, and find creative ways to overcome problems. I want a position that would involve finding marketing campaign ideas and working with project teams."

This touches on various areas of the candidate's experience, all of which relates to the job they are applying for. This answer makes it easy to see why they should be considered for the position.

Now, not every one of these questions will have an example of a bad way to answer them, but we have provided an example with this question. It is always a good idea to know what a bad answer looks like. This example stems from applying for the same job as the above good answer:

"I hail from Montana, and I am very outdoorsy. I grew up fishing and hunting, and I still try to get away and do that when I can. I graduated from Montana State where I ran track. I moved to Denver, where I became a Broncos fan. I love watching their games, and I hope they get to the Super Bowl this year. I am married with two kids. My oldest is a bookworm and does very well in school. My youngest takes after me and has a passion for sports."

While this does allow the interviewer to get to know them, it won't help them in getting to know if they would work for the position. It did not include any relevant work experience, career accomplishments, and it didn't explain why they are there for the interview.

How would somebody who doesn't like you describe you?

Why are they asking this question? The person conducting the interview wants to know how you handle an unexpected question and makes you realize you aren't perfect.

Address the answer. Don't avoid by stating that everybody likes you. Be careful not to give any negative feelings about yourself but think about various work styles and why somebody who has a different work style might not like you:

> *"Wow. That is a great question—since I normally don't focus on negativity or think about others not liking me professionally. But if I must answer: the person who didn't like me would say that they don't like working with me because I like to take things as they come and face a problem, while they like to think things through too much. They like to create plans and analyze the situation completely before they dive in, and that frustrates me."*

Do you have any regrets?

Why are they asking this question? Everything is not going to go your way all the time, and the interviewer wants to know how you handle things when something goes wrong.

Address the question. Give a regret you might have that would be relevant to the job in question and the things you learned from it:

> *"I am not a person who focuses on things such as regret—since everybody makes mistakes. It is important to address the mistakes and move on. If I have to focus on an answer, I would have to say that I regret not being open to other opportunities earlier in my career. While I was in college, I was super-focused on the kind of job I wanted. I knew the*

role, industry, and location. Once I received a call to be interviewed, and it wasn't located where I wanted, I declined the interview—since it wasn't where I wanted it to be. I have learned not to be closed-minded to opportunities. Now, I am used to commuting for about one hour."

What would you do differently if you had to relive the past ten years?

Why are they asking this question? The interviewer wants to see where you are going with your career by asking you to reflect on the past.

Try to focus on what you have learned over the years and if you had known then what you know now, would you have done anything differently?

"I am not the kind of person who lives with many regrets. I try to be thoughtful about my actions, but everyone makes mistakes. One thing I would have done differently but could have only learned through the experiences that I have lived through was to be more culturally sensitive. I have worked with a lot of people from various backgrounds, and I could have understood their perspectives based on their experiences better. I think we might have worked better together."

What would your dream job be?

Why are they asking this question? The interviewer wants to know if your goals and dreams will line up with the organization's.

Try to focus on job duties that are relevant to the job you are applying for. Try not to name a certain job title. Try to paint a real picture:

"I try to look for potential in most things. Regarding the jobs that I have had, all of them have had parts of my dream job. I

know that even the perfect job is going to have stress at times along with various challenges—both small and large—that I will have to overcome. The ideal job for me is when I constantly contribute to the media organization in a progressive, meaningful, and responsible way."

Are you a follower or a leader?

Why are they asking this question? The interviewer wants to know how your role will fit into their organization.

Each organization will value leadership qualities, but they want a person who follows directives too. Try to keep a balance between the two of them:

> *"I take a leadership role on occasions that call for experience or expertise that I have and that other colleagues might not possess. I am always ready to share my knowledge. As a leader, I know that it is important at times to be able to follow and learn from other people."*

What Was Your Favorite Job?

Hiring managers love to find out what your favorite job was. This gives them a sense of what you enjoy, and it tells them whether you would be a good fit for the role you are applying for.

When you have to answer this question, pick jobs that have similar attributes to the one you are applying for. You better be prepared to answer why you left the job as well.

We are going to take a look at a simple answer for a person applying for the job of an arbitrator. Some of the responsibilities that this job may include are guiding conversations to a mutual agreement, clarifying issues for involved parties, and facilitating communication disputes between parties:

> *"I was a student counselor in high school. I loved how challenging the job was. Students came to me with different*

types of issues, most of which had to do with conflicts between faculty, family members, or friends. This is where I found that I loved helping others work through conflict. It was extremely rewarding getting to help my fellow students resolve their issues in a way that helped both sides. This is why I pursued a degree in counseling. Now, I am looking for a job where I can begin my career and my passion for helping others work through their problems."

This answer shows that the person has a real passion for the role in which they are applying for. It also lets the employer know that they have taken concrete steps to prepare for their desired role.

If you are presented with this question during a job interview, think of a job that you had that helped to prepare you for the job that you are applying for. Then make sure that you highlight the attributes that show your skills and passion for the job. If it isn't obvious, make sure that you explain why you chose to leave the job. In this example, there is no need for an explanation since it would be implied that they left after they graduated from university. If you don't have an obvious reason, make sure you address the reason.

What Was Your Least Favorite Job?

This can be a tricky question to answer. It could be that the interviewer is trying to find the things that demotivate you. They are looking to make sure that you aren't going to be turned off by some of the main elements of the position.

It is best if you pick a past job that is completely unrelated to the position you are applying for. The majority of us have held a job that was a terrible fit for us. Choose from one of those jobs, and explain why the new job you are seeking is a better fit for you.

We are going to look at a sample answer from a person applying to be a waiter or waitress. Some of the responsibilities of this job could be taking payments, preparing checks, answering questions about the menu, and greeting customers:

"I worked as a bookkeeper during summer at a small resort. I am pretty good with numbers, so I felt that the job would be a good fit for me. However, it turned out not to be. I love working with others, and I like getting to move around at work. As a bookkeeper, I had to sit at a desk all day and had no interaction with others. While I was there, I also had a job as a waitress at the resort's hotel. I loved working those shifts because I got to interact with others. I also got to move around as I worked. I want to find a role where I can work around others and move around during the workday. Hopefully, my skills with numbers will help out since I will be taking payments."

The best part about the answer is that the candidate focused on the positive parts. It is very easy to allow yourself to focus on the negative parts of your least favorite job. You don't want to allow yourself to go into the negative because the employer won't like that. You can use this question as a means to turn an unappealing job into a positive experience.

Who has inspired you and why?

Why are they asking this question? Since the person doing the interview doesn't know you, they want to understand what helped to make you who you are today.

Give them some examples of mentors, friends, or family who have inspired you through their dedication and work ethic:

"It would be difficult not to be inspired by a person's parents. Thank goodness mine served as great role models. In addition to dedicating all their free time to their children, they had a tremendous work ethic. My father would get up very early to get to work earlier so he could put in extra hours so he could get home to see his children before they went to bed. If he had to, he would return to work after we went to bed.

My first supervisor, Jane Hughey, was also an inspiration to me. She had a great moral compass. If something appeared questionable, she taught us to lean toward the right thing to do. She was right since it strengthened our relationship with clients and benefited everyone involved in the end."

What tools and techniques do you use to stay organized?

Why are they asking this question? In this world of ever-increasing demands, reporting, and multi-tasking, your interviewer wants to know how you stay organized.

Everybody had various strategies, but try to paint a picture of a person who is organized and has made a system to remain on top of the work:

"The first thing I do is make a running task list for myself in Google Docs. Within that list, I place deadlines and notes as to how I am progressing. I have a calendar app for all my appointments and to-do lists as well as a physical appointment calendar as a backup. I like to get to the office early to clear my inbox and voicemail and make a solid working plan for the day."

What's your personal mission statement?

Why are they asking this question? The interviewer wants to know what defines you so they can determine how you will fit into the company.

Give them a well-defined statement that demonstrates your strong drive to succeed, moral compass, and work ethic. Think about the company's mission statement and be sure that it is compatible with yours.

> *"I will use my strong work ethic and drive to succeed so I can meet my objectives, as well as those of the people who count on me, in a responsible and morally appropriate way."*

What's your greatest achievement other than work?

Why are they asking this question? The interviewer wants to know you as a person outside of the job setting.

Try to focus on an achievement that shows your abilities, skills, or experiences that you performed outside the job:

> *"I have been volunteering for Habitat for Humanity since 1999. When I began, I was only a helper when we went and helped to build a home. I have worked my way up and am now a team leader. It is a great feeling to lead others successfully in volunteering their time for such a worthy cause."*

Tell me something about yourself that you don't want me to know.

Why are they asking this question? The interviewer wants to know how you will handle a question that you have not anticipated and what you might say.

Never give them an actual weakness. Give them something that you might not have said but made you feel like a strong candidate:

> *"Well, to be honest, I have been following this company for some time now. I am a big fan of your work. I know you do not want to hire a fan. You are looking for someone who is a great fit as an employee, and I think that I am an excellent balance between the two of them."*

What is your favorite teenage memory?

Why are they asking this question? The interviewer wants to understand more about you as a person.

Give them something that shows you have good character and makes you a better professional.

> *"My favorite memory was watching my sister graduate from high school. She struggled with math and was not even sure she would graduate. I tutored her, and she grew confident. A couple of months later, she copied her diploma and sent it to me along with a thank you note."*

Do you want to be feared or liked?

Why are they asking this question? The interviewer wants to know about your management style.

Try to find balance in the middle ground. If you say you want to be liked, they might think you are just a pushover. If you say you want to be feared, you are going to sound like a dictator:

> *"I would want to be liked since I am a respected leader who leads by example. Since I am an effective leader, my team would be fearful of not doing their best since each would know that everybody has to put in their best effort and nobody wants to be a disappointment to the team."*

What is your favorite quote?

Why are they asking this question? When the interviewer asks for your favorite quote, they are trying to get a better insight into who you are.

Quotes can be powerful. The way you interpret a quote can mean different things to different people. Try to select something that is not too personal or makes you seem like you lean toward controversial topics. Try to select something about strong work ethics or leadership. Tell them why you chose it and what it means to you:

> *"I heard this as a teenager while I was still figuring out what I wanted to be. It is a quote by Bruce Springsteen: 'My parents always told me to get a little something for myself. What they didn't know was that I wanted everything.' This inspired me to reach higher for my goals and not to settle. I knew that it wouldn't be easy, but if I maintained a strong work ethic, I could achieve what I wanted."*

Do you have a role model? Who? Why?

Why are they asking this question? Since the interviewer does not know you personally, they want to know what made you who you are today.

Give an example of a mentor, friend, or family member who was your role model through their dedication to task and work ethic:

> *"It would be hard not to get inspired by your own parents. Mine served as great role models for me. They did not just dedicate their time to us; they also have a great work ethic. My father would get up early and go into work early so he would get off earlier and be home in time for supper and to tuck us into bed. If he had to, he would return to work after we had gone to bed."*

Whom do you respect? Why?

Why are they asking this question? Showing respect for others is a part of any job. Your potential employer wants to know if you respect others.

Let them know you respect everyone and can work with anyone as opposed to somebody needing to earn their respect:

"I think it is important to respect everyone. Although some people might seem to be more accomplished than others, and worthier of respect, we do not know everybody's story and how they got to be who they are. When we begin on an even playing field of respecting everyone, without feeling that somebody has to earn our respect first, we are more likely to make stronger bonds and better working relationships."

Whom do you admire? Why?

Why are they asking this question? Since the interviewer does not know you, they are trying to understand what made you who you are today.

Give an example of someone who has inspired you through their dedication to task and work ethic:

"My first supervisor, Margaret Creson, was an inspiration to me. She had a great moral compass. If something was the least bit off morally, she taught us always to go toward the correct thing to do. She was totally on-the-spot that it strengthened our relationship with clients and benefited everybody."

Would you refuse to work with anybody?

Why are they asking this question? The interviewer wants to know the type of people you will and won't be able to work with.

You have to show them you are open to working with everyone. If there are specific personalities that might be a challenge for you to work with, you will still do what it takes to make it work:

"Since I am not a CEO, it is not my choice to say whom I will or won't work with. I always do my best to make things work. Now, are there going to be difficult personalities at any job? Sure. Whom do I prefer not to work with? If I had to say, the two types of people who come to mind are the ones

who are know-it-alls and those who are liars. It is hard to have open communication with those types of people. I will always trust the company to put them in the right roles since they do contribute to any organization and I will figure out a way to make it work. The most important thing is having open communication when I encounter a problem. I would ask for open dialogue to clear the air."

What would you actually want to do in life if you got to choose?

Why are they asking this question? The interviewer is trying to figure out if this job is going to fit into your plan. It helps them assess how happy and successful you will be in their company.

Make sure your answer is in the context of the job that you are interviewing for. Make an impression of what you want to do and how this job might help you reach it:

"I have always loved advertising. The exact role is not as important as the opportunities involved in all the different aspects of the business, including being creative. This role will be a wonderful opportunity to contribute what I know, improve my track record, learn more, and hopefully take on more responsibility."

Give me an example of a time in your personal life when you were dishonest with somebody.

Why are they asking this question? The interviewer wants to know about your moral character.

You have to admit that you have lied before, but give them an explanation as to why it was the right thing to do at the time:

"A long-time friend made a mistake at work, and the company fired him. He wanted to know if it was going to hurt his ability to find a job. I knew that it would, but his

confidence was gone, and he was feeling bad that he let his family down. I lied and told him that it might not hurt his chances."

What traumatic experience have you experienced in your personal life?

Why are they asking this question? The interviewer wants to know how you handle things when times get tough.

Give them an experience that was hard to deal with without getting too personal. Keep your answer focused on the way you dealt with the experience:

> *"Thank goodness that I haven't experienced any traumatic events that would fall outside the regular circle of life. I was very close to my grandmother growing up, and she passed when I was just 13. It was very difficult. It happened at a time when I was transitioning into my teenage years and thinking about her became a moral compass for me.*
>
> *As I had to make difficult decisions, I would think about what she might do in similar situations, and it made decisions clearer for me."*

Name the most important thing that you have learned in life.

Why are they asking this question? The interviewer wants to know something that has made you who you are today.

Give them an important lesson that you learned, what happened that caused you to learn it, and how it is relevant to the job you are interviewing for:

> *"No matter what situation you are in, you have to be true to your values. During my first week on a new job, I was asked to fabricate some records on behalf of the company. Since I*

was counting on this job to support my family and give me a solid footing in the field, I started doing what I was told. I began not sleeping well and was stressed about having to do this. I realized this did not fit into my values no matter what the consequences. Thankfully, the company respected my wishes, and I did not have to do something I didn't want to. It reinforced for me that I don't ever have to do something that does not fit into my values—no matter what."

What do you fear the most?

Why are they asking this question? The interviewer wants to learn more about your personality.

Explain why you have a particular professional fear and the way it relates to this job:

> *"Professionally, it would be somebody thinking that I am not doing my best. I have a very strong work ethic, and I give it everything I have. I would be very disappointed if somebody trusted me and felt like I was not doing my best."*

Do you think it is necessary to make new relationships?

Why are they asking this question? Networking and building connections are essential to any business. The interviewer wants to know how you build and establish your network.

Tell them why it is important to nurture and build relationships. Give them examples about how you established a relationship and the way it benefited your employer and yourself at the time:

> *"I believe that it is not just worthwhile but essential to building relationships. If you just lean on the relationships you have established in the past, your network will get smaller each day, as people retire or move to another company. When using resources like LinkedIn, it is easy to*

reach out and establish new relationships. I have several examples, but a quick email exchange with a wholesaler in Ireland help open that market up to our company."

How Would A Friend Describe You?

This gives you a great chance to highlight your best attributes. As always, make sure that you demonstrate the abilities you have that would make you effective in the job that you want.

Think about the other people that you work with, and think about the way they would describe you. What types of characteristics would they say you have that would make you a good fit for the job? Are you a good listener, creative, collaborative, inspiring, or friendly? Now, choose some of those characteristics that relate to your career goals, and then tell the interviewer a story that illustrates your abilities to use those characteristics to get results.

We are going to look at a simple answer for the job of a radio talk show host. Some of the responsibilities for this position would be entertaining their audience, interviewing guests, commenting on current events, and announcing radio station programming:

> *"My friend would say that I am entertaining, possibly, the life of the party. In college, I would always tell stories to friends while at lunch. Once, my friends dared me to record one of my stories and post it on Facebook. I created the video and posted it. In a couple of days, it had gotten over 2,000 views. I then uploaded it to YouTube and made my own channel. When I came up with a new story, I would record it and post it to my channel. As a result, I have more than 11,000 subscribers, and my videos have received more than one million views. I want to get to use my ability to entertain others as a sports reporter. I love sports and being able to entertain others. Since my YouTube audience and my friends tell me I am good at it, I'm here to make it happen. I invite*

you to check out my YouTube channel to see if you agree with
my friends, and then decide if I am entertaining enough."

While entertaining is not a characteristic that fits many jobs, it is right for a position in the entertainment industry. When you are preparing for your interview, it is best to pick relevant characteristics, and then share a story that shows how you used this skill.

Be Professional

The majority of interviews will start with questions about your work experience. Interviewers use these questions to figure out if you have the basic skill set that is needed for the job. If you make sure you know how to answer these questions, the easier the interview will be; otherwise, it can end up being quite difficult when you aren't prepared.

These first questions help you set the tone for how the interview will go. They will also allow you to set yourself apart from the other candidates. Let's go over how you should frame your answers for these questions.

First off, the interviewer will probably be talking to dozens of other possible candidates. Many of them aren't going to leave an impression. When you frame your answer properly, you can make a lasting impression so that they view you as a top choice.

Start by letting the interviewer know something that you are passionate about, but make sure it relates to the job you are applying for. They are looking for people who enjoy what they do, so make sure you let them know what you enjoy. Here are some examples:

- If you are applying for a job as a graphic designer, you could say something along the lines of "I love when I get to be creative."

- If you are applying for a salesperson job, you could start out saying something like, "I like to build relationships with others."

- If you are applying for a job as a bookkeeper, you could say, "I love to organize. I enjoy organizing things into neat groups."

Now take a look at some job-specific details for the position you are applying for and try to figure out what passions relate closely to the responsibilities you would have.

Next, make sure you summarize the experience you have. This needs to be brief and does not start going into a lot of detail. This will let your interviewer have some context for the remainder of the interview:

- If you are applying to be a marketing manager, you could let them know, "I received my bachelor in marketing from NC State. Once I graduated, I started working at Hush Ad Agency where I was in charge of creating digital media campaigns."

- If you are applying to be a cashier, you can tell them, "I have helped two different retail jobs during the last eight years. I was an assistant cashier at Michaels before being promoted to head cashier. From there I worked as a head cashier at Kmart."

- If you are applying to be a police officer, you could say, "I have an associate's degree in criminal justice. I worked as a security guard at an office building while in college."

Take a look at your resume and see where you have work experience that relates to the job you want. Then take some time summarizing the experience you have.

Next, you will want to let the interviewer know what kind of experience you would like to learn. You need to make sure that your answer is directly related to the job you are applying for:

- For an office manager, you could say, "I want a job that will let me use my organizational skills while also providing me chances to supervise others."

- For a financial advisor, you could say, "I want to reach a position where I can grow my knowledge in the realm of estate planning and retirement."

- For a teacher, you could say, "I would like a position where I can create lesson plans and teach English—since English is my subject of choice."

Now let's take a look at question-specific answers.

Walk Me through Your Resume

This is very much like the first question in the first chapter. When it comes to this question, it is best to summarize every section of your resume. Provide the interviewer with highlights from your experience and education sections. It is best to share this information in chronological order.

Fight off the temptation to read off of your resume. They do not want to hear you reciting things that they could simply read for themselves. They want to hear things in your own words.

We will look at a good answer for a person applying for a job as a medical sales representative. The responsibilities for this job could include creating relationships with PCPs and selling medical supplies:

"I have a passion for building healthy relationships. When you look at my resume, you will see that I have a bachelor's degree in chemistry from Northern University. While I was there, I was elected as the president of the debate club. I

believe this shows that I can build strong peer relationships. I am also persuasive. After I graduated, I got a job at Mill Labs, where I worked as a lab assistant. That is where I learned my passion was in selling ideas, not lab work. The director of sales saw my passion and provided me with the chance to prove myself in the sales department. My performance in sales was in the top ten percent, and I was promoted from assistant sales rep to associate sales rep. I am now looking to move into a role that gives me more responsibility for a wider range of products. I want to be in a place where I can create lasting relationships with customers and help them to succeed using the products that I believe in."

This answer shows that the applicant has a lot of background knowledge for this role. They also make sure to explain why they are looking to switch careers.

What major problems and challenges did you face at your last job?

Why was this question asked? There are many challenges in a job. The person doing the interview wants to know how you handled challenges and problems in past jobs since you will probably face some challenges in this job too.

You have to show the ways you can overcome a challenge. Give them an example of a challenge or problem that has relevance to the interviewer and shows the ways you overcame the problem. When you structure your answer, give the challenge and follow with the actions and results:

"Two years ago, my employer acquired a niche firm. This created natural friction between long-time employees and the ones who were hired during the acquisition. Every team had their way of doing things. In the beginning, having more employees slowed down the ability to get projects finished

successfully because of conflict and miscommunication. After this, I asked my team members to meet me for lunch. We went to a relaxed atmosphere and started discussing the way we work and why we do it this way. It opened up a line of communication, and we started understanding one another better. This led to better teamwork."

Do you have any leadership experience?

Why are they asking this question? Since the ability to lead is important, and it does not matter what your role is, the interviewer wants to know about your ability to lead by finding out what you have done in the past.

Give them a memorable story or two that will show leadership qualities. It is best to give them a couple of stories than to give a list of all your experiences, with none of them being memorable for the interviewer:

"Each quarter, my department provided a report on its accomplishments to the executives. I volunteered for the team leader in gathering the information from coworkers and making sure that it was as organized and accurate as possible. I called several team meetings to set objectives and deadlines for our work and met with individual members to answer any questions and to make sure we were on the same page. We produced a report that was praised by the executive team, and I have been the go-to person ever since."

What accomplishment gave you the biggest satisfaction?

Why are they asking this question? This shows your ability to get things done. Showing what you have accomplished in the past shows how inclined you are to accomplish things in the future.

Give the interviewer an accomplishment that is relevant to the job you are interviewing for. Paint them a picture of things you have accomplished, how you went about accomplishing them, and why they were important to you:

> *"I have always been great at multi-tasking, but I was not sure that I would be able to go to school full-time while working and raising a family. It wasn't always easy, but I was able to do it successfully. I would study on the train, wake up early, go to sleep late, and learned how to manage everything that I do more effectively."*

Have you used your creativity to work through a problem?

Why are they asking this question? Nobody has a book that tells them how to solve any problem that will come up at work. The interviewer just wants to know how creative you can be to solve problems.

Give examples that are relevant to what you are applying for. Describe the problem, the approach you used, and what the result was:

> *"I have to establish relationships with executives. The hardest part is getting in touch with them. I have learned how to find any email address at a company when you can find that of one person. I Google for an email address of anybody at that company to figure out how their system works. When I find an executive's name, I can get in touch with them directly. This has given me a higher rate of responses than just trying to reach them by phone or an intermediary."*

What technical skill has helped you most?

Why are they asking this question? An ever-increasing skill is a technical aptitude no matter your role. The interviewer just wants to get a better understanding of what your strongest skills are.

Give them a technical skill that is relevant to the job you are interviewing for. Show your expertise by giving them an example of the way you used it and why it was successful for you:

> *"I have an understanding of how to utilize social media. I have trained sales staff to use LinkedIn to increase a company's visibility."*

Have you developed or learned any new skills recently?

Why are they asking this question? The interviewer wants to know if you like learning throughout life. Companies are looking to hire people who want to learn and not just stay stagnant.

Give examples of something you have recently learned that is relevant to the job you want. Tell them how what you learned is relevant and what you have accomplished:

> *"I recently learned more about how important body language is. It has helped me to identify what people are trying to communicate with their bodies even when they are saying something different. This skill has been helpful with going to business meetings and establishing new relationships."*

What types of things have you accomplished to be more qualified for your career?

Why are they asking this question? The interviewer wants to know if you will learn new things over the course of your career. Companies hire people who like learning and aren't stagnant.

Give an example of how you continue to improve and learn to be a better learner:

> *"I believe it is important to keep learning so I can improve. I try to participate in as many professional development opportunities as possible. I attend two or three conferences a year in my field. I participated in cross-training from other departments at my current job. Additionally, I am an active contributor in several relevant LinkedIn groups."*

How have you improved your knowledge in the past year?

Why are they asking this question? The interviewer wants to know if you like learning over the course of your life. Companies want to hire individuals who are always learning and aren't just stagnant.

Give a few examples of how you continue to improve and learn to be a better learner:

> *"I believe that it is important to continue to learn so I can be better at my job. I go to as many seminars as I can fit into my schedule during the year. I make sure that some of the seminars have something to do with other departments at my job, so I am cross-trained if I'm ever needed to help out elsewhere within the company."*

Do you have any unique experiences that separate you from others?

Why are they asking this question? The interviewer wants to know the reasons why they should hire you rather than someone else.

Try to focus on building yourself up rather than knocking other people down. This is the time to give yourself a huge boost:

> *"I cannot speak for other people, but I know why I am a great fit for this job. I'm the right choice because I have 15*

years of experience taking on a progressively responsible role in my field. I have exceeded objectives and helped to grow the business. I have been asked to represent the company, assist wherever needed, and train others. I constantly learn and keep improving my skills by taking advantage of all relevant, continuing education opportunities. Even though I have a history of success, I still try to reach new goals and overcome challenges. I have followed your company closely for several years. I know that we can be great partners in success."

Give me an incident that happened in your life that shows the way you faced a challenge and the way you dealt with it.

Why are they asking this question? Each job is going to have its challenges, and the interviewer wants to know how you will handle it.

Give them relevant examples of an incident that happened on the job, the way you handled it, and the result:

"When you are helping clients, you can only do your best, but you cannot make everyone happy all the time. There was one client who felt I was not doing everything I could to help. She came into the office screaming. I was able to calm her down, and she met with the president of the company. He gave her the opportunity to complain. I had documented all of the work I had done with her and was able to show the way I provided her the same service as I had with other clients. We heard later that she was dealing with other problems. This gave me the chance to strengthen my relationship with the president and explain how I worked."

Why were you given a promotion?

Why are they asking this question? The interviewer wants to learn how you were able to move up the corporate ladder so quickly.

Talk about all the accomplishments that allowed you to get the promotion. Emphasize the accomplishments that are relevant for this job:

> *"I was promoted from account manager to trainer within one year. This was because of my stellar sales record while maintaining and growing accounts, along with my ability to lead others and train them to work efficiently."*

Did you acquire any skills from your internships?

Why are they asking this question? If you have just graduated from college with only limited work experience, the interviewer wants to learn what skills you might be able to bring into a full-time position.

Try to focus on the skills that you gained from an internship that is relevant to the job you are interviewing for:

> *"The most important skills that I learned were to manage my time, pay attention to detail, and work effectively within a team."*

Have you ever had to give a person difficult feedback and how did you handle it?

Why are they asking this question? When you are in a management position, you might have to talk with a subordinate or coworker about a difficult problem. The interviewer wants to know the way you would handle it.

Give them relevant examples that tell the story up to needing to have the conversation, what was talked about during the conversation, and how it ended:

"It is never easy to provide somebody with difficult feedback but to work effectively you have to do it at times. It seemed like a friend or coworker was letting their hygiene habits slip. They went from wearing nice outfits to stained clothing. It looked like they were not showering. I had a private conversation with them and mentioned how the other coworkers had noticed how their habits had changed and were getting concerned. They explained that they have become overwhelmed with becoming a new parent and hygiene wasn't on their radar like it had been in the past. They said they would take care of it. They did change the way they dressed and cleaned up. I am glad I told them since it could have cost them their job."

Have you called in sick to work for more than a couple days with any job?

Why are they asking this question? The interviewer wants to know the type of work ethic you have, and how much time you come to work will give them some clarity.

If you do not regularly take off work, explain some times that you did and why it was important to you. Give some clarity into your work ethic:

"I always felt that when I was absent from work, I was missing out on something, so it was very rare that I would take time off at all. The only time I can remember, with the exception of vacation time, was to help care for a family member after they had surgery."

What Do You Do to Be More Effective?

When an interviewer asks you this question, they want to see if you are motivated to make improvements to your skills. Interviewers want candidates who look to learn more and find more ways to be better at their job.

We will look at a good answer to this question for the position of a creative director of a flower shop. Some of the responsibilities for this position could be designing floral displays, meeting with clients, and training staff on floral designs:

> *"I love finding ways where I can express my creativity and share ideas. I like to look through Daily Motion, Vimeo, and YouTube each day to find new floral arrangement designs. I also keep up with several bloggers, and I am now producing my own videos that teach others how to arrange flowers. You can see my videos on YouTube. Next, I would like to have a team that I can train to do floral designs so that we can always have new ideas to help delight our customers."*

This answer lets the interviewer know that you love the work you are applying for so much that you are constantly looking for new ways to do your job better.

Tell Me about a Time You Demonstrated Great Leadership

When your interviewer asks you to tell them when you demonstrated great leadership, they are interested in hearing that you can get people to follow you. This skill involves having the ability to understand the things that motivate others and teaches them to trust you. It also includes being able to communicate well in ways that make other people want to follow you.

The story that you come up with for this one, and it should be a true story, not fiction, can be modified with some variations for any of the following:

- Tell me about a time you demonstrated:
    - Leadership
    - Teamwork
    - Persuasion

We will look at a sample answer for the position of a shift manager at a restaurant. Some of the responsibilities for the job could include resolving customer issues, assigning tasks, and leading the operations of the restaurant when the manager is not present:

> *"While a cashier at Top Sirloin, two of the employees started screaming at each other. There was not a manager around at the time, so I decided to step in. I immediately told them to follow me to the back office so that they would not upset the customers. Since I had gotten along with both of them, they followed. I was able to get them to calm down and tell me what was going on. I persuaded them to be patient, and wait for the other to tell their side. It all turned out to be a big misunderstanding as they had each thought that the other had intentionally bumped into the other. Once they realized it was just an accident because they were both trying to do the same thing, they calmed down and agreed to get back to their respective tasks. Once the manager came back in, I told them about what happened and that I had helped to resolve the issue. As a result, they both learned to trust one another. They work well together and are now good friends. This incident got me a promotion to restaurant shift manager."*

This answer shows that an important part of being a leader is listening to others. An interviewer likes to hear that you can motivate others by listening to what has happened and then helping them come to a mutual solution that helps them and the company.

We are going to take a quick look at a bad way to answer this question. We will stick with the position of shift manager:

"Since elementary school, I have been a great basketball player. While in high school, I led my team in rebounds and points. I was also a leader on a Boy Scouts hike. We hiked to a beautiful national park, and I was the fastest. In fact, the other kids had a hard time keeping up with me. I also led my debate team to the most wins. I am extremely competitive, so I worked hard to beat my other team members. If I get hired, I will bring this competitive spirit. I will look for ways to beat my coworkers at any goal that is set."

First off, they are rambling with several examples that do not relate to the position. The best answer would be one that focuses on how they can motivate other people.

Also, they do not have a good grasp of what leadership means. Instead, they like to be a better team member than others. They don't focus on how to build a team to achieve a goal; they try to do it all on their own. This does not show that they would be a great team leader.

Tell Me about a Time Where You Demonstrated Great Creativity

For any position that would require out-of-the-box thinking, the interviewer is interested in hearing examples of how you have come up with creative solutions to interesting problems. They want an example of how you can create ideas that nobody else has thought of, and how you delivered this idea.

We will look at a sample answer for the position of a public relations manager. Some of the responsibilities could be leading social media efforts, writing press releases, and developing public relations strategies:

"When I first started work at the Northeastern University's Theatre as their PR Coordinator, the attendance was low. I

was supposed to increase attendance to the plays. I took a look at other entertainment businesses to see who did the best at marketing. I found that movies generated more awareness because of their trailers, so I thought the theatre could use this. I talked a friend, who was majoring in visual arts, into helping to create a trailer for one of the plays as a project for her class. I then ran the trailer on the social media networks for the campus. The trailer ended up getting over 2,500 views, and the attendance went up 50 percent. We surveyed the attendees, and over 65 percent said that they first heard about the play from our trailer."

If you work in a creative field, but you do not have any examples that show this type of creativity, take some time to look through video sites. Those sites will provide you with many different creative ideas. For example, with some research, you can learn how to use videos to promote just about anything. The interviewer would be impressed if you let them know that you have posted tutorials for topics that you are interested in, which could easily be helping to drive awareness to charitable organizations to help tutor children.

Tell Me about a Time When You Demonstrated Good Collaboration

The majority of jobs are going to require you to work well with other people, so an interviewer is probably going to want to know of a time when you demonstrated this skill. There are different words they can use for collaboration questions. These include:

- Ability to work with difficult people

- Interpersonal skills

- Collaboration

We will look at an answer to the position of a computer programmer. Some of the responsibilities could include integrated work with coding from different programmers and writing code applications:

"I worked at Pixelcon Gaming, and we were working on a new video game. I was supposed to write code for the vehicles in the game. Halfway through the project, the project manager and creative director could not pick an ending. I was in good standing with them both, so I talked them into having a war room session with me. During our session, I led a brainstorming exercise so that they could share their ideas. We were able to come up with several different ideas that hadn't been considered, and one of them turned out to be the option that we went with. In the end, we were able to agree on the best solution and completed the project on time. That game is now a best seller."

When it comes to collaboration questions, the interviewer is looking to see that you can get others to work together towards a common goal. They want to know that you can listen to several points of view and then discover the common ground.

Tell Me about a Time Where You Demonstrated Great Analytical Skills

If the job you are looking to get requires analytical skills, the interviewer is going to want to you know how well you can use data to make decisions. There are a few ways that this question can be worded. They include:

- An ability to use data to make a decision

- An ability to think strategically

- An ability to solve complex issues

- Analytical skills

We will look at an example answer for the position of an innovation director for a sporting goods store. Some of the responsibilities would be determining market potential and identifying new product lines:

"I worked at Top Shot Sporting Goods as an innovation manager. I was required to assess and identify business opportunities for a new line of sports equipment. While attending my son's martial arts tournament, I saw hundreds of children wearing sparring gear, so I started to look into this as a new product line. During my research, I found out that more than four million Americans participate in some type of martial arts. These people spend, on average, $200 annually on equipment. That is about $800 million in retail opportunities. With the average markup being 50 percent, the wholesale opportunity is about $400 million. This information helped me to persuade the executive team to approve a test for a line of martial arts gear. We ended up creating a new product line that has been delivering more than four million dollars in sales each year. With just a one percent market share, they have more room to grow."

When it comes to analytical questions, the interviewer wants to see that you can discover relevant data and use that data to make the best decisions. They want to see that you can conduct research and make realistic assumptions when needed.

Your Best and Your Worst

These are the questions that everybody hates to get. While everybody knows, deep down, what their strengths and weaknesses are, we all seem to struggle with answers to questions about them. You can guarantee that there is going to be a question from this section asked in your interview. If not, it is a miracle.

The interviewer is looking to see: one, if you can be honest, and two, if you can do the job they need you to do. Nobody truly wants to share about their downfalls, but you don't have to focus on the negatives of them. They can be learning experiences, and that is how you should answer these types of questions.

When presented with a question that seems to have a negative answer, you should answer it in a way that puts a positive spin on it. When you get asked a question that has a positive answer, make sure you keep yourself humble and do not come off as cocky. A person who cannot see the good in a bad situation or somebody who thinks too highly of themselves is not somebody that the company is likely to hire.

Tell Me about a Time Where You Regretted a Decision You Made

The interviewer could ask you about a decision that you regret to see if you can learn from the mistakes you make. These types of questions give you the chance to show your ability to adapt to changing environments and use your experiences to become more efficient.

With these questions, provide them with an answer that highlights a key skill that comes from the job description. This will make sure that your interviewer will see that you learned from past experiences and that the odds of you making the same mistake are slim if you are to get hired.

We will look at an answer to this question for the position of a strategy director. Some of the responsibilities for this job could be developing recommendations for business models, managing teams of consultants, and leading strategic projects:

> *"I worked as a strategy manager at Capital Bank. I was assigned to write a project brief to prep our consulting company for a new project. The project required creating a new strategy for improving customer satisfaction. The brief I wrote used a template that the bank had used in the past for consulting projects. The consulting firm assigned their own teams of finance experts, but they did not have anybody on their team that had customer research experience. This meant that their initial recommendations involved cost-cutting measures, but they didn't address the main objective, which was to help satisfy customers. I realized that there needed to be a new approach, so I spoke with their project leader. I asked him to work with me to come up with a new brief so that I could find the skills they needed for the assignment. Because I saw the mistake early on, I helped the consulting firm find a person with the expertise required for*

the project. I also needed to revise the company's brief to include 'required skills' so that we would not have this problem in the future. The financial team estimated that the new brief would help save the bank around $100,000 each year in consulting fees since the projects would be staffed with people with the skills required. From this, I learned that every project is unique, and I have to make sure to evaluate the scope of each project so that team members with the right skills will handle the needs of the project."

This is a great answer because the candidate has shown that they learned something from a mistake and discovered a way to make sure it did not happen again. When you prepare for a question like this, make sure you find an example that shows how you can improve the company once they hire you.

This will let the interviewer see that you are the best choice because you do not just make a mistake and move on; you learn and then help others to avoid this same mistake.

What's your biggest failure?

Why are they asking this question? Everything is not always going to go your way. Your interviewer needs to understand how you handle things when something doesn't go right.

Address the question. Never avoid it by stating that you have never failed—everybody has failed at something sometime in their lives. Give a relevant failure and tell them what you learned from it that makes you who you are today:

"Early on in my career, I stressed myself out trying to grow my capabilities. I worked full time and was going for my master's degree nightly and on weekends. I was able to manage it until I got a promotion at work. I began feeling overwhelmed and quit the master's program when the semester ended. It made me feel like a failure since I could have taken more time to work out the responsibilities. I have

learned to think things through better now before I make final decisions. Just to note: I have restarted my master's program, and things are going great!"

How do you define failure?

Why are they asking this question? When you work a job, it is all about meeting goals. The interviewer wants to know how you judge things such as failure and success.

Give them some insight into the way you work so that it will be appealing to the interviewer:

> *"To me, failure means you are not even trying. At times there will be opportunities that a supervisor will give that a person can accept if they are willing to take on the challenge. Most people are afraid of failing so they will not even try to take on a challenging assignment. For me, not trying something just because it is out of my comfort zone would be failing."*

What is your greatest weakness?

What are they asking this question? The interviewer is asking this question to get to know the professional you better. They do not want to only hear about the things you do well but what you don't do well.

Give them a weakness that you have had, what you did to overcome it and how it has affected your life:

> *"I have always thought of myself as a quiet person. I am very comfortable talking to others one on one or giving presentations. I have always felt intimidated when introducing myself to people I do not know. Because of my role in the business world, I knew I had to get over that. I've made a great effort to get myself out there and meet new people. Yes, it is intimidating to do this, but I don't think that*

anybody has noticed that I am uncomfortable at times and I have made some great connections."

If a former manager were to ask you, what three things would they want you to improve on?

Why are they asking this question? The interviewer is asking for you to be honest and share some professional aspects about yourself that might be your strong points.

Try to focus on facets about yourself that might have been ways to improve yourself early in your career. Tell the ways you overcame those weaknesses and where you are today:

> *"The supervisor at my first job had a harsh personality, so I have a fairly good sense of the way to answer this one. They would say:*

> *"'He has bad communication skills—He thought that I could not communicate well and shouldn't be allowed to answer the phone. I felt this was because I am a quiet talker when getting used to a situation. I have taken steps to improve my communication skills. I've been going to toastmaster meetings for five years now. This has improved my public speaking, and this is a major part of my job."*

> *"'He has limited technical know-how.'—When I began that particular job I was not experienced in using a computer, so it was a difficult learning curve for me. When I became comfortable using technology, I took to it very well. Now, I enjoy doing podcasting, blogging, social media, etc.*

> *"'He is not a leader.'—I know why my first boss had this perception of me. As mentioned, I was quiet and intimidated easily. I only focused on the work. Since then, I have grown as a professional, and my leadership abilities have grown too. While doing that job, I helped train new employees and was in charge of running the office when the supervisor was*

out of the office. I have grown in my career, and taken on the role of team leader."

What accomplishment are you proudest of?

Why are they asking this question? The interviewer wants to learn what you have accomplished in your past. When they know this, they will know what you might accomplish in the future.

Try to paint them a picture with words of what you accomplished that is relevant to the position that you are applying for:

> *"I was called upon to do a job that was meant for two people. I met the demands of both positions, but to actually excel—since the company acquired many new businesses— the CEO was looking for a person who had experience in account management to lead a new team. They asked me to do it while keeping my old position too. I would spend about two and a half days at each place per week. By maximizing resources, especially using technology to communicate, I stayed on top of each role and went above and beyond expectations."*

How do you deal with stress?

Why are they asking this question? The interviewer wants to know how you manage stress since work is normally stressful.

Be honest about getting stressed. Give concrete examples to show the way you manage stress:

"I try to prioritize my time and stay calm when thinking about what I need to do first. If it is a stressful time of year, I make sure to spend lunch away from my desk and get some exercise. I find it makes me feel refreshed, so I have the energy to deal with work."

How do you balance work and life?

Why are they asking this question? The interviewer wants to find out if you are a well-rounded person.

Give good examples of ways you maintain the balance. They will be unimpressed if you tell them that you cannot maintain the balance and you are a workaholic:

"It is difficult to keep the proper balance, but I think I manage it very well. For me, the key is maximizing my time. On the train to work, I prepare for work, and while going home, I am preparing for the next day. By doing this, I can mitigate the need to stay late at the office and spend time with the family. The weekends are family time unless there is something essential that I have to take care of before Monday rolls around."

Are you competitive?

Why are they asking this question? Many jobs require a specific amount of competition, either externally or between employees. The interviewer wants to see how well you handle things.

Give them clear examples that show you love competition, but you will not do anything unethical just to get ahead:

"I enjoy healthy competitions. I find that competing with coworkers motivates all of us to do better. If somebody comes up with a great technique or strategy that works well, the next person can build on that, and everyone can grow."

Name your best skills.

Why are they asking this question? The interviewer wants to know the skills that you would bring to the table. This is important for them to know when deciding on whether or not to hire you.

Try to focus on skills that are most appropriate for the job you are interviewing for. You cannot just simply name your skills like you are making a grocery list. Take this time to explain how proficient you are in each skill for the job:

> "I am great at communicating. I present my ideas well in person, through social media, and in writing. I have worked hard to sharpen these skills because I feel the value of a great idea is pointless if I can't present it in a way that others can understand.
>
> I am a real team player. There is no room for a "me first" attitude in the workplace; we all have to work together in order to meet objectives. When I have completed my work, I will walk around my department and ask coworkers if there is anything I can do to help contribute."

Tell me about a time you made a mistake due to you not listening well to what you were told.

Why are they asking this question? Everyone makes mistakes from time to time. The interviewer wants to know if you learned anything from them and how you fixed them.

Own up to your mistake. Tell them what you learned from it and how it made you a better worker:

> "I was asked to run a comparison of sales month to month and create corresponding charts and graphs for a presentation. I jumped in with both feet. I was so excited to show it to my boss until he informed me that he only wanted me to run comparisons for the past three months and not for the entire year. Unfortunately, I had wasted a lot of company time by putting in all the extra information and not working on anything else. I learned to pay attention next time and confirm what my supervisor wanted before I started."

Have you ever had to make a difficult adjustment? What was it?

Why are they asking this question? There is going to be constant change in the workplace, and the interviewer wants to know how you can handle it.

Give them examples of change/s that you have done relevant to the job you are interviewing for. Tell them what the challenge was, how you overcame it, and the result:

> *"Change can be hard, but I am always ready to embrace it. Within my industry, one skill that is important to have is an ability to engage clients one on one and build rapport to strengthen relationships. My company asked everyone in the division to stop all in-person meetings and start doing what we do over the phone or computer. It was hard at first to build rapport without being face to face. As I shifted into relying on new methods of communication, I created new strategies for beginning conversations with clients remotely. In the end, I have been able to interact with more clients using the new strategy, and I find that I'm now able to engage clients as well remotely as I can in person."*

Have you ever misjudged someone?

Why are they asking this question? The interviewer wants to know if you can interact well with others since this is an important part of any job.

Give them a clear picture as to why you misjudged someone, what happened, and how it was resolved:

> *"I try not to judge people that I do not know well, but it could happen occasionally. There was a new person who joined our division. He seemed to be moving extremely fast to get noticed by upper management. He set up meetings with*

vice presidents and started giving reports on how well we were operating. What I did not realize was that he was new to this industry and he didn't know the communication protocol that was in place. When he realized, he was very embarrassed and started being a team player. He is very humble and was not looking to step over anyone."

What did you learn from your mistakes?

Why are they asking this question? Everyone will make mistakes, and the interviewer just wants to know the way you learn from them.

You have to admit to your mistakes and explain what you learned. Tell them how it made you a better worker:

> *"Early in my career, if I got overwhelmed with work, I would try to work as fast as possible to keep up. This caused me to make a mistake on a spreadsheet. I left out some valuable data, and I submitted it like it was. When I became clear that I messed up on the report, I realized that it was better for me to take my time and do the job right instead of rushing."*

Describe a time when you weren't pleased or satisfied with your performance. How did you fix it?

Why are they asking this question? The interviewer wants to know if you take your work seriously and if you hold yourself accountable.

Give them an example that is relevant for the job you are interviewing for. Tell them about the work you did, why you were not satisfied with it, what you learned, and how it helped to improve you:

> *"I was asked to run an analysis on a competitor. I examined all of the important metrics. My supervisor was satisfied with the report, and they told me it was helpful in making*

investment decisions. While I was learning more strategies for running a report like this, I got embarrassed at the quality of my work. I realized I should have included competitors in related markets and not just direct competition. I learned to lean on senior analysts to give me their feedback before I submit a final report."

What criticism have you received that was most useful to you?

Why are they asking this question? The interviewer wants to know if you can take constructive criticism and the things you have learned.

Give them examples of criticism that somebody gave you that is relevant to the job you are interviewing for. Be clear about what you have learned:

"While in college, I planned to go into the live events marketing field for my career. In an interview for a summer internship, the director suggested that I reconsider my interest in the field as I would have to commit many evenings, weekends, and travel to the position. In considering what I wanted from a career, I refocused my efforts toward brand marketing, and that has been a better fit."

What do you think you are good at doing?

Why are they asking this question? The interviewer is trying to know what your greatest strengths are along with your confidence level.

Give them examples that are relevant to the job you are interviewing for. Focus on a few things that you might not be great at, but you have worked hard to improve on:

"I think that I am a natural listener and give helpful advice. Other aspects that I am good at did not come very easily. I have worked hard to learn them, but now I think I am very

strong. Those skills include knowledge of spreadsheets, writing reports, and making presentations."

Have you ever had to make a decision without having all the information you needed?

Why are they asking this question? Each job will require you to make judgment calls without having all the information. The interviewer wants to know how you have handled decisions in the past so they can understand the way you handle things now.

Give them an example of a decision you made that is relevant to the job you are interviewing for. Tell them about the entire process, what decision you made and why, the way it turned out, and the result:

> *"In the e-commerce space, we have to make predictions as to what items will be in demand during the holiday buying season. We look at past sales figures and interest in certain products to predict, but it can be hard to figure out. Normally, it has worked out fine, but there were some years it did not. The first few years I was involved, we took a hit, but I was able to build in better metrics to learn from our mistakes and improved things in the future."*

If I were to ask a previous supervisor what your strongest point is, what would they say?

Why are they asking this question? The interviewer wants to know if your strengths match the job you are interviewing for.

Try to focus on one strength that they would value on this job. Give them an example of how you have used the strength successfully:

> *"My supervisor would say that my greatest strength is my can-do attitude. Somebody could have all the skills in the world, but if they are not willing to give it their all, every day at any time for anyone, then those are not great skills. I am*

always willing to do my best and help out as I know that it is all about meeting company goals."

What is the hardest part of being a (job title)?

Why are they asking this question? The interviewer wants to consider what the hard parts are about your current job and if it is relevant to the position you are interviewing for.

Try to focus on something difficult that you have dealt with that is relevant for the position you want. Tell them how you overcame the challenge:

> *"To me, the hardest part of my last job was firing people. Every time I had to let someone go, I had butterflies in my stomach the whole time. At times, I would be nauseous. I want the company I work for to run as efficiently as possible. When a team can come together and do that, everyone can help each other and support their families. There will be times when a person will not fit into the dynamics of the company anymore, and we have to let them go to make sure we have the best company out there."*

What is Your Greatest Strength?

This should be one of the easiest things for you to answer during your interview, but some candidates provide answers to this question that do not relate to the role that they are applying for. There are also people who provide a short answer without connecting it to the job. For example, if you are interviewing for a marketing position, you may say that your greatest strength is organization. This would be a great answer for a person who wants to be a bookkeeper, but it wouldn't be all that great for a marketer.

You want to give the interviewer a strength that is directly related to the role that you want. Then follow up your answer with an example of where you used that strength to get results. Here are a few strengths and jobs that they align with:

- Doctor – diagnosing and treating complex illnesses

- Salesperson – can build strong relationships

- Manager – can lead people

- Accountant – attention to detail

When you answer a question like this, pick strengths that fit the role you are applying for. Then provide them with an example of how you have made use of this strength to get results in your past positions.

We are going to look at an answer to the role of a psychiatrist. Some of the responsibilities for this job could include treating and diagnosing people who have emotional or cognitive challenges:

"I have always been great at listening. While at my residency, my supervisor consistently said that my listening abilities were exceptional when it came to discovering important details that others would often miss. There was one time when my supervisor asked me to interview a woman who had received an OCD diagnosis to see what the best treatment would be. While interviewing her, she mentioned that she had trouble in high school. I asked her some questions to get more information. Eventually, she finally revealed that she witnessed a friend get hurt in a serious accident. I discovered that her symptoms started shortly after this. With this, I corrected her diagnosis from OCD to PTSD. Since I was able to listen carefully, I was able to catch onto something that the other doctor had missed. I fixed the diagnosis so that she didn't end up living with the wrong diagnosis for years. This helped the treatment team get her on the right medication, and she has now become a great mother, married her husband, and can hold down a job."

The interviewer is looking to hear about a strength that makes you perfect for the position you need to fill. When you look over the job description, think about the things you do exceptionally that match the description. Then, come up with the best example of when you used that skill.

What is Your Biggest Weakness?

Interviewers will often ask this to see if you are self-aware. A person who tells them that they do not have a weakness comes off as arrogant or hard to work with. If you share a weakness that is actually a strength, you are going to look insincere.

The best way to approach this question is to share a weakness that you have managed to work through or a weakness that is not related to the job you are applying for.

We are going to look at an answer for the role of a sales vice president. Some of the responsibilities that this job could include are making changes to the organization of a department, determining training and recruitment needs, and leading sales strategies:

> *"I have typically been better at focusing on the big picture instead of the small details. When I started working as a salesperson, that issue ended up causing problems for me. For example, I had to sell a pet food line to a major retailer, and they wanted to have exclusive pricing deals for each item. I tried to handle the complex pricing plan, but it was hard to get every part correct. Fortunately, this taught me to get my financial counterparts involved when it came to transactions that needed more attention. With this experience, I have learned how to build better relationships with others who are strong in areas that I am not. My most valued colleagues are my financial counterparts. They value the fact that I am great at building customer relationships and create sales strategies that work, and I value them for their ability to manage all of the little details. As a result, my team has been able to increase the company's sales over the last three years."*

This is a great answer to a tough question because it shows that they are effective in the role they are interviewing for. A sales vice president is not going to be involved in the small details, so it is perfectly okay that they are not a detailed person. However, it is a good thing that they recognized their weakness, and they know how to compensate for it.

If you get presented with this question, make sure you are honest with your answer, but provide an answer that still lets them know that you are the best choice for the job you are there for. Also, it helps to show how you have learned how to overcome or compensate for weaknesses, either by bringing other people in to help or creating a process that overcomes the problem.

Do You Know Them?

These questions are asked to see how well you know the company. These questions help them to know if you are ready for the position and if you are fully aware of the responsibilities you will have in the position. Some of these questions can be framed like we have framed some of the previous questions concerning your passion, experience and what you want to do next.

Then there will be some that will use the 30-60-90 day plan framework. We explain that framework in the next chapter because it deals with more time-based questions.

These questions are the reason why we suggested you research the position and the company. You do not want to be caught off guard with these questions by being completely unaware of what the company does and what you are supposed to do.

What is the First Thing You Will Do?

If you get asked this question, your answer should never be, "PARTY!!!" The interviewer does not want to know how you are going to celebrate getting the job; they are looking to find out whether or not you are going to have an immediate impact or if you are going to need a lot of hand-holding and training to help you get up to speed. It is important that you show them that you are ready to hit the ground running.

We are going to look at an example of this question for the position of an office manager at a doctor's office. The responsibilities for this job could include training staff, assigning clerical tasks, and organizing office operations:

"I am glad you asked. I have taken the liberty of drawing up a 30-60-90-day plan so that I can show you my thoughts on how to approach this job. During the first 30 days, I would like to get to know everybody in the office and hear what suggestions they have for the best way to approach my role. This is also when I would like to learn your process for maintained medical records, billing, and booking appointments. During the next 30 days, I would like to find and implement a few things to make sure that our office culture stays strong. I also want to find ways to improve our processes. Then, in the next 30 days, I would like to make sure the staff members get the training that they need to be effective in their position. I would also like to make some changes in the roles for staff members based upon their interests and capabilities. Here is a copy of my plan. Would you like me to change anything?"

When you end your answer with a question, you will move the interview into a problem-solving mode. You are letting the interviewer know that you understand there is always room for improvement and you are inviting them to help you improve. If they do engage and start helping with your plan, then they are going to want to see you succeed.

Let's take a quick look at what a bad answer to this question would look like. We will still be using an office manager position:

"Well, I guess your billing system is going to be awful, so I will have to fix that. A friend of mine is a bookkeeper, so I would ask her to help me create a better billing system right

off the bat. Then, I would ensure that the staff is aware of what I want them to do. I am strict on how I run things, so I would expect my staff to come in early and stay productive throughout the day. I would also expect all tasks to be finished before they leave for the day."

This is an overly aggressive approach and would definitely alienate employers. However, then again, they could have answered the question like this:

"I would like to get to know everybody in the office. I think it is important to have friends at work, so I would want to have lunch or coffee with each of them. Then I would come up with some team building exercises. Maybe we could travel offsite to a company retreat. I think this would help the staff to get to know who I am."

While team building is a good idea, so is accomplishing work. It is important that you can find a balance between getting to know your coworkers and having an impact.

How Did You Hear About Us?

This probably seems like a simple and harmless question that should have a short answer. However, this is a great way to distinguish yourself from others. If other people gave the quick answer of, "I found the job listing on LinkedIn," you have the chance to impress the hiring manager with an answer that shows how committed you are to their company.

We will look at an answer to the question for the position of a teacher. Some responsibilities for this question include maintaining an orderly classroom, teaching students, and creating lesson plans:

"I always wanted to teach at a school that has a strong community. I have been working as a substitute for the North Buncombe School District for the last three years. I have been trying to find a school where I have the chance to

become a full-time teacher since I have an education degree from West University. I have not been a substitute at your school yet, but many of my colleagues have. They have told me how amazing your staff is here. I have also read about your progressive approach to lesson plans, and I like what I have seen. I have also taken the time to read through your Facebook feed and website, and I love how you have built up the community. I discovered your job listing because I regularly review your job postings in the hopes of finding an open position like this. Through my research, I believe that this is the perfect place for me to become a valued member of your staff."

This candidate did quite a bit of research before they headed into their interview. This is much more impressive than telling somebody you found the job listing on craigslist.

Before you head into an interview, take some time to look over: the company's website, social media feeds, recent news articles about them, and try to talk to others who have worked for them. This is going to set you apart from others who have applied for this job.

Interviewers love it when you show them that you have put some effort into the job search, especially when the effort has been targeted towards their company. It shows them that you are more likely to stay with them if you have done a fair amount of research needed to determine that they are the right fit. Therefore, provide an answer to this question that has details about your job search.

What Do You Know About Us?

They are asking this to find out how interested you are in the job. If you do not provide a good answer to this question, the interview is pretty much over. Make sure that you show them that you are really interested in the job.

You can make sure that you are ready for this question by doing your research about the company before you go into the interview.

Look through their website, Google them, and look at their LinkedIn profile:

Here is a good answer if you are applying for the position of an accountant:

> *"Your firm was founded in 1988 by Robert Adams and Jessica Stewart to provide corporate and auditing services as well as other regulatory reporting and compliance. The firm now has more than 300 employees with a great reputation. Some of your clients are top companies from around that state. There are offices in three major cities, and the company seems to grow consistently. I read an article where Jessica Stewart in Accounting 101 talked about the results of the research the company has done into effectively reporting data accurately through a mobile app. This is very interesting research because I know the importance of accurately reporting and collecting such data, especially for helping management be effective."*

You don't want to overdo your compliments. Show them that you have done just enough research to know that you understand and are interested in working with the organization, but try not to come off as a "stalker".

Your Future

Interviewers will often ask these types of questions to gauge the kind of interest you have with the job that you are applying for. They want to see if you plan on being with the company for many years, or if it is a stepping stone for you.

For some of the questions, you can use the same type of framework we have talked about before where you cover your passion, experience, and what you want to achieve next. For others, it is best to use the 30-60-90 framework. This framework outlines how you see yourself during the first 30, 60, and 90 days on the job.

If you present the hiring manager with a well-thought-out 30-60-90-day plan, you will blow them away. Even if all of your ideas are not completely in line with the company's specific situation, you will still impress them with the fact that you took the time to think through your first few months. Here is how you can work out a 30-60-90-day plan:

- 30 – Talk about how quickly you will meet your coworkers, define your priorities, and learn about the business.

- 60 – Show how you could begin to show results and influence projects that are related to yours.

- 90 – Show how you could start to lead initiatives with importance to your department and create new ideas to improve the business overall.

How soon do You Want to Make an Impact?

This question will often be asked to see if you are prepared to hit the ground running. The interviewer may be looking for immediate results, and they want to know that they can count on you to do that.

This is a great question to use for the 30-60-90-day plan framework. We will look at a good answer to this question when applying for the job of an events planner. The responsibilities for this job could include managing event timelines, negotiating contracts, and developing agendas:

> "I plan on having an immediate impact. I have been an event planner in this area for eight years, and I know all of the local agencies and venues. I have written up a 30-60-90-day plan to help show how I would approach this—should you hire me. During the first 30 days, I would like to get to know everybody within the company who is involved with the big events. I want to learn from them how the event planning has been handled in the past and then we can talk about ways to improve it. I want to start working on an event immediately so that I can learn through real-world experience. In the following 30 days, I want to manage more complex events progressively. I would also like to start using some improvements to make the planning process easier and to make them even more impactful. In the next 30 days, I would like to look over the contracts and capabilities for the agencies that are normally involved with the events. I would like to see if I could notice any capabilities that we have not been leveraging or opportunities to help us save money. Here is a copy of my plan. Are there any changes you would make?"

This answer shows an eagerness to learn during their first 30 days. Then, they have a clear plan to take on more responsibilities the longer they are in the position. It lets the interviewer know that the interviewee understands that there is a learning curve involved when they join a new organization, and they want to learn quickly.

What are your goals?

Why are they asking this question? They want to know if your goals will line up with the organization.

Try to focus on an approach where everyone wins as opposed to just what you want. Be specific about the relevant items in the industry that you want to accomplish but do not name certain job titles:

> *"I would like to continue to contribute to the media organization in a very meaningful way. My job title is not as important as the work that I do. I know that if I positively contribute, the company and everyone will benefit and win in the end."*

Do you have any short-range objectives and goals? Why? When will you make these goals? And how are you preparing to achieve them?

Why are they asking this question? The interviewer wants to know how your goals match up with the company's goals.

Think about the job that you are applying for and give them an answer that would be great for anyone in the role:

> *"I would like to move from my role as a Media Buyer into a Senior Media Buyer. This allows me to meet some of my short-range goals of being able to contribute to the company more dynamically, learning about the buying side of the business, and having an opportunity to mentor and train junior employees."*

Name one important goal you set for yourself in the past and how did you reach it?

Why are they asking this question? Reaching your goals is important in any job. The interviewer is using how you accomplished this in the past to see how you might do things in the future.

Tell them a goal that you successfully reached. Give them a description of the way you went about reaching this goal, including challenges that you overcame:

> *"One goal I had was to secure business meetings with 500 marketing managers in one year to introduce them to a new web tool. The challenge was that nobody at my company had been able to have a meeting with more than 200 people in a year since there was a very limited travel budget. I made a plan that helped maximize my time and reach. Utilizing technologies such as Skype, I was able to interact with my target audience one on one without leaving my office, and this saved valuable time. When I had to leave the office, I used a relevant conference as a hub and to meet with as many people as possible. I would then travel around the conference location and meet with local people, so I did not have to make separate trips. To build up my contact, I asked each one that I met with to introduce me to someone new. Not only did I reach my goal but I exceeded it. I ended up meeting with 540 marketing managers last year."*

What Are Your Future Goals with the Company?

This can be a tricky question. You want to show the interviewer that you want this job and that you would like to move up the ranks once you get it. However, you also want them to see that you have normal, realistic expectations. This question can go in either direction. Some people have shown that they will be complacent within the role and others show that they have too much ambition—which makes HR think that they will constantly be demanding promotions. You want to make sure that you can express the right combination of eagerness for growth and willingness to put in the time.

Let's take a look at an amazing answer for the position of an architect. Some of the responsibilities for this job could include researching building code, preparing project reports, and creating building designs:

> *"I want to become a highly-skilled commercial architect. From my resume, you can see that my certifications and education have provided me with a solid foundation. My immediate goal is to become part of an architecture firm where I will be able to continue to build on my foundation. I want to learn more about CAD applications, building code requirements, and project budgets. I want to be a part of a firm where I can apply my experience and grow the number of my responsibilities with time. I want to become a Project Manager or Senior Architect, and then, hopefully, become a partner. I know this will take several years, but I am committed to doing this."*

This is a perfect answer because it shows that they have the willingness to work in order to reach their goals. They also did their research on the architect career path. This also shows that they have a good balance between willingness to put in the work and a desire to progress at a reasonable pace.

You want to stay away from an answer that could end up making you seem unmotivated or overly ambitious. If you let the interviewer know that you do not have any specific goals, they are going to view you as unfocused or lazy. If you let them know that you plan to be running the company in just a few years, then they aren't going to take you seriously.

Can You Handle the Heat?

Also known as behavioral questions, interviewers ask these questions to see if you would be a good fit for the company. They want to learn how you can approach different situations, and make sure you can do it in a compatible and acceptable way.

To answer these questions, you should frame it with the STAR method.

You start with the situation. Use one sentence to describe the situation. This could be simply restating the scenario they gave you or telling them where you last worked and your job title.

Then you will talk about the task. This is a sentence to tell the interviewer what the assignment was or what you would have to take care of.

Next, you will use a few sentences to explain the action steps you took to address what happened.

Then you wrap it up by telling the interviewer the results you got from the action you took.

It is always a good idea to think up five or six stories before your interview to fit different types of questions. With the right types of stories, you can be ready for a wide variety of questions. For example, it's a good idea to have some stories that fit into the following areas:

1. Analytical – this would include your ability to problem solve, think strategically, and apply mathematics in order to deliver results.

2. Collaboration – this would include creating relationships and demonstrating interpersonal skills.

3. Creativity – this would include thinking outside the box and discovering new solutions to fixing problems.

4. Leadership – this would include creating a team, getting results, and being persuasive.

5. Persistence – this would include staying focused, working hard, and showing determination.

6. Flexibility – this would include knowing how to manage your time, be adaptable, and prioritize.

Tell Me about a Time When You had to Demonstrate Flexibility

An interviewer will likely want to know about a time when you had to deal with a challenging situation. They could be looking for somebody who can manage competing priorities and work on vague projects.

We will look at an answer to the job of a civil engineer. Some of the responsibilities that this job could have include monitoring the progress of projects and planning constructions projects:

> *"I worked at ABC Construction as a civil engineer. At one point, I was handling three projects, and all of the project managers wanted me to work full time on their projects. I met with the managers to talk through the timelines and figure out which project was the most urgent. I found that one project would not receive its materials for six months, so I*

talked the manager into moving his timeline out a couple of weeks. On another project, I was able to delegate some of my drafting work to a junior member. Then I turned my focus to the most urgent project with tasks that only I could perform. I followed up with the junior member to make sure that they were making good progress in their work. Once the projects were finished, I turned my attention to the third project that had not been as urgent. By delegating and prioritizing, I completed all of the projects on time. One of them even came in under budget because I delegated some of the work to a person with a lower billing rate."

Interviewers love people who know how to prioritize their work. They are also looking to find a person who can keep their managers informed as they make work decisions. It is important that you craft your answers related to time management, prioritization, and flexibility to show all of your skills while making sure that your manager agrees with how you approached the problem.

When did you last get angry?

Why are they asking this question? The interviewer wants to know how you manage emotions while on the job and if you can stay professional.

Address the question—do not try to tell them that you haven't ever been angry. Give them a good example and share what you learned from the experience:

"As a professional, I try to stay away from being angry at clients or coworkers. There might be times when somebody might do something that upsets me, but I try to manage my emotions. An example does come to mind. Early on in my career, I had to share a cubicle with a person who had a similar job as mine. I try to be all about my work and being a professional. This person was only there for the paycheck. He looked at inappropriate websites, made personal phone

calls, and even fell asleep when meeting with clients. The last meeting was very upsetting since it was not just him appearing unprofessional—it caused me to look bad too. He was eventually reprimanded, and I was able to take on more responsibilities and move away from being associated with him."

Have you ever helped resolve a dispute between coworkers?

Why are they asking this question? Strong personalities and conflicting opinions are a normal part of the workplace. People who can take on a leadership role and resolve problems are of great value.

Give the interviewer an example that demonstrates your ability to lead and resolve problems. Tell them what the problem was, what action you took, and what happened in the end:

> *"While I was an accounts manager, I was a mentor to two new employees. They were closely working together, and a problem came up as to which one got the credit for landing the new account. They agreed to talk it out with me before talking with the supervisor. After they heard each other's side, they agreed that they each deserved some credit and realized that to find mutual success within their new roles, it would be best for them to continue to work together."*

Have you ever had to make a hard choice between your professional and personal life?

Why are they asking this question? The interviewer wants to know how well you balance your personal and professional life.

They do not want you to tell them you will always prioritize your professional life. Give an example of a hard situation that might relate to the job you are interviewing for. Tell them how you resolved the situation with mutual benefits:

"It is hard to keep a balance between one's personal and professional life. Since my daughter is a toddler, she is usually in bed by 7:30 pm. I would normally get home while she is awake. I know it is not always possible, so my spouse and I have devised various ways to make it work. If I know I am going to be at work late, I might wake up an hour earlier to spend time with the baby. I will talk with my supervisor and find out what work has to be completed in the office or what I can do at home, so I don't have to stay late. At the time, just talking about it with my supervisor helps. When I began my new job, they required all employees to work two days every week in overtime. After about six months, I explained to my supervisor that clients often came in late on one of those nights and so suggested being available earlier one morning a week for client convenience instead. This change helped me be more effective professionally and allowed me to spend more time at home."

What happens if you cannot solve a problem by yourself?

Why are they asking this question? The interviewer wants to know how you handle problems that are above your abilities.

Tell them the process of knowing that the problem was beyond your expertise area and how you found somebody to help you:

"I have served clients in many different regions of the world, but the needs of the banking industry in Australia were uniquely unfamiliar to me. I quickly did my best to acclimate to their needs, but I knew that I could not gain the level of expertise needed in only a few days to compete for the account. After I talked with my supervisor, I reached out to our division that was based in New Zealand since I know they would have a better idea of the industry culture. We

partnered to gain the account, and it worked out great for everyone."

Have you ever persevered over a difficult problem to make sure you had a successful outcome?

Why are they asking this question? Each job will have its challenges, and the interviewer wants to know the way you will handle it.

Give them relevant examples of a problem you encountered while on the job, and the way you handled it and what the result was:

> *"In the very first week on a job, I realized that data had not been tracked in an effective way for many years. I found paper files with information that was different from the online databases. It was a horrible mess. I was not sure I would be able to dig myself out and start to focus on the job's main tasks. Thankfully, I had been working for some time at this point, and I had enough confidence that I would be able to get things organized—eventually. I sped up the process by coming in one hour early, working through lunch, and staying an hour late to get the project organized. I spent my normal working hours concentrating on the main job at hand."*

Tell me about a problem you had to solve in a different way. How did it turn out?

Why are they asking this question? Each job will have problems that need to be solved, and the interviewer wants to know how you take a different approach to solve them.

Give them a problem that was facing your company that you helped them solve along with the different approach you used. Describe something relevant for the job you are interviewing for:

"Due to some executive management mistakes in the past, my company had the perception of being a regionally-based service provider. Because there was no budget to make an advertising campaign, I used my knowledge of social media to spread the word and gain traction in other markets. It was successful, and the company has accounts outside of the region."

Your boss brings you a lot of work at 3 pm and tells you she needs them by 5 pm, but you know there is no way you can get it done in just two hours. What will you do?

Why are they asking this question? The interviewer wants to know how you will manage an unrealistic or unreasonable task.

Give them a strategy that shows them you are a team player and will do whatever it takes to achieve the objective, but you are also capable of giving them a realistic viewpoint when it might be impossible to meet that objective:

"I would tell my boss that I will clear my calendar for the remainder of the day and do my best to complete as much of the work as possible. I would also give insight that I think it will take longer than two hours to complete, and ask if it is a hard deadline. If it is not, I would stay late if necessary to complete it. If it is a hard deadline, I would ask the boss if I could ask some coworkers, whom I know would be able to contribute as well, to drop what they are doing so that we can work on this together and complete it by the deadline."

How would you go about telling your boss they are 100 percent wrong about something?

Why are they asking this question? The interviewer wants to understand how you can handle sensitive topics about management while keeping with protocol.

Tell them that what you would do all depends on the situation while keeping your respect for management:

> *"I would handle it depending on the situation. If it is something inconsequential to my job, my boss, and the bottom line of the company, I would have to think about how my boss would handle being told that they were wrong and possibly let it go. If it were something that might affect the company's productivity and the company's ability to meet goals, I would ask to talk with the boss privately. I would want to tell them their information was wrong in a meeting. I would explain that I trust their information, but that in this case, I believe they are wrong and why. I would leave it up to the boss to decide what to do with the situation."*

Could you fire a person if you had to?

Why are they asking this question? The interviewer wants to see if you can make difficult decisions and hold a management position.

You have to prove to them that you can handle difficult tasks. Tell them why you can handle it:

> *"Well, in this role, I know that I will have to make some hard decisions. It is a stomach-churning experience to have to fire someone. When it does not feel like that, somebody probably shouldn't do it. With the way I manage, I am looking for my company to run as efficiently as possible. When we are doing that, we can help all of the employees at the company to*

support their families. From time to time, people no longer fit, and we have to let them go to help the company run as efficiently as possible."

Tell Me about a Time Where You Remained Persistent

Interviewers like to find out if candidates can show that they can continue working hard and stay persistent during challenging situations. To assess their abilities, an interviewer could ask any variation of questions like:

- A strong work ethic

- A willingness to go the extra mile

- An ability to handle a difficult situation

- Persistence

We will look at a sample answer for the position of a physician assistant. Some of the responsibilities for this job could include consulting with physicians on the treatment, performing exams, and interviewing patients:

"I worked at the Chicago Hospital as a physician's assistant. There was a patient who came into the clinic with a shoulder rash. She had already seen four doctors, two of whom were allergy specialists, and none of them was able to help her. I met with her and took note of her complete medical history. I asked her about her home and work environment. I then started researching some possible causes of the rash. I also talked to her daughter, who had just come back from Madagascar. I was able to find an article about a rare allergic reaction that was caused by a fabric made from a Madagascan plant. I referred her to a doctor who specialized in rare allergic reactions. He confirmed that the rash was caused by a shirt that her daughter had brought back from

Madagascar. Through my research and assessment, I was able to diagnose something that four other doctors missed. I love being able to solve problems like this, and I will do everything I have to in order to learn the cause of a patient's issue."

Interviewers are looking to find out that you are willing to go the extra mile to get your job done. By giving this kind of answer to a question like this, you will make yourself stand out from the other candidates.

Tell Me about a Time When You Had to Address Competing Priorities

This is the perfect question to see if a candidate can prioritize a tough workload. When it comes to this question, the interviewer is looking to find out if you can make good choices and also keep your supervisors informed when you have to make tradeoffs.

This also shows them if you can delegate work when possible and choose the project that needs your attention right away over the one/s that can wait. We will look at a great answer to the position of administrative assistant. Some of the responsibilities for this could include performing administrative tasks, preparing an expense report, and scheduling appointments:

"At my current employer, I help the vice president of sales. Last month, I was getting ready for the national sales meeting when my boss gave me an urgent request from our CEO to host a market tour for a board member. I reached out to three of our regional sales directors to see if one could host the tour. One of them was excited about the opportunity, so I had him plan the tour. I spoke to the CEO's assistant to work with the sales director on the tour details. I had them copy me their plans so that I was able to let my boss know what was going on. For the sales meeting, I recruited a sales analyst who was interested in meeting planning. She was

able to help me find a venue, coordinate the presentation, and manage the attendee list. During all of this, I sent regular updates to my boss about the meeting and the tour. Since I found a way to delegate the work for both projects to team members who really wanted to help, both projects ended up being a success. We surveyed the meeting attendees, and the meeting was rated as one of the best in the last ten years. After the tour, the board member sent a glowing report to the CEO. The CEO said that this tour was the main reason why my boss was promoted to Senior VP of Sales and Marketing. I am proud of this because I love to see a person that I support get promoted."

The conclusion of the answer was great because it shows that the interviewee is happy for others when good things happen. Since the interviewer could be your boss, they will be able to make the connection that you could help them achieve more success in the company.

This shows that the candidate is flexible. Employers like people who can adapt to the ever-changing circumstances of the workplace by locating others to help out on projects.

What is Your Tolerance for Risk?

Interviewers will ask this question to see if your tolerance for risk is in line with the company's culture. The answer will depend on how your possible employer views risk.

There are some industries, like high-tech, where risk is very much encouraged as part of their development process. There are other industries, like the medical field, where risk should be avoided at all cost.

We will look at an answer to the position of a computer software developer. Some of the responsibilities for this job could include implementing patches, testing software, and designing computer game applications:

"I love when I get the chance to take risks. These risks allow me to learn and expand my skills. For example, a couple of years ago, I was helping develop a first-person shooter game. I was assigned the task of designing weapons for the game. The original specs called for standard weapons. I felt like it would be more interesting to see if I could design the bullets so that they exploded on impact. I spent a couple of days researching the coding that was used to create the explosion in a car crash in a racing game. After some failed attempts, I was able to replicate those effects in the game we were working on. I was able to create a weapon that we called 'The Zombie Killer', and it came with an intense explosion effect that was better than any other weapon in the game. This weapon I created was the main reason why our game was rated number one for first-person shooter games."

Now, we will look at another answer that would be appropriate for a job that would not want you to take risks. This answer is for a pharmacist. Some of the responsibilities could include instructing patients on how to use their medicine, verifying the physician's instructions, and filling prescriptions:

"I take careful steps to avoid risks. In the pharmacy world, risks can end up have life or death consequences. For example, a couple of years ago, I was finishing up my residency in a small pharmacy. I had to double check prescriptions to help reduce the risk of adverse reactions. Since they did not have an automated system for detecting these problems, I offered to find them a program that could help. I did some research to find the best software. When I found a good software, I came up with a beta test to make sure that it worked correctly on their computer system. During the next six months, we checked to make sure that the software detected the possible adverse reactions on each of the prescriptions. During our beta test, I found that the software didn't work well with the computer system. I

persuaded the owner to invest in some new computers so that the software would work correctly. I finished the beta test to make sure that the software was going to work. As my residency came to an end, the pharmacy underwent an audit, where the FDA reviewed the prescriptions filled for the last three years. They found that after we started using the software, the number of possibly harmful drug combinations went down by 80 percent. Since I was so careful, the pharmacy became a safer place to fill prescriptions."

It is easy to see that you need to make sure that your answer to a question like this is tailored to the role you are seeking to get. During your research, you should be able to tell if risks are encouraged within your chosen field. You should also try to find out if anybody in the company can provide you with an indication of how they perceive risks.

If they encourage risk taking and you like risks, let them know that. If they discourage risks, and you are careful, let them know. If your view on risks does not line up with the company's, you may need to pass on that job and try to find a position and company that aligns better with your views. There is nothing more frustrating than working somewhere that is not a good choice for you.

What Are You Looking for?

This group of questions will let the interviewer know what you expect to get if given the job. This gives them an idea of how reliable you would be when it comes to scheduling as well as what you are looking to get when it comes to salary.

While this does not seem like something you can research, you can actually do a lot of research for these questions. You should make sure, beforehand, that your salary, vacation, schedule, and benefits needs can be met by the company. If not, then you should move to a different company.

If you feel that they will be able to meet your needs, then get some answers prepared for these types of questions. The framework will vary with each of these answers, but many of them will use the framework that we have used in previous sections.

When Would You Be Able to Start?

If you make sure that you are properly prepared, there is a good chance that your interview can end with the question, "When can you start?" Even if this question does not get asked, you should make sure that you are prepared for it—since, hopefully, it does come up shortly after your interview.

You want to answer this truthfully. Of course, all of these questions should be answered truthfully, but for this question, candidates will more often than not respond with the answer they think the interviewer is interested in hearing instead of giving a realistic answer. If you still have to give your current employer two weeks' notice, then let them know that.

Also, it is perfectly okay to ask when the interviewer wants to fill the role. If they are flexible with the start date, you can negotiate a little. They may be good with delaying if you state that you are willing to take some time off between the old and new job. You are not going to learn this if you don't ask, so much sure you do. They prefer somebody who is not afraid to get all the information. Here is a great way to answer this question:

> *"Did you have a specific date in mind that you would like to fill this position by? My current employer requires that I give them two weeks' notice, which I can do as soon as we negotiate the details of the offer. However, if you are looking for somebody to start later, I am willing to go ahead and give my notice and then take some time off before I start working with you. Let me know what works for you."*

This is a perfect answer because it shows that the candidate is interested in the job, but it also shows that they expect to negotiate an offer. You want an interviewer to be interested, but you do not want them to get the impression that you are willing to accept any offer. Given the chance, you need to let them know you will accept the right offer and that you want it to be fair.

Why isn't your salary higher at this point in your career?

Why are they asking this question? The interviewer wants to know how much salary matters to you in your career goals.

Tell them about your strategies to prepare yourself for the highest possible earnings as opposed to just taking whatever job comes next that offers more money:

> *"Up to now in my career, it has been about contributing to the organization and getting all the experience I can. I did take some jobs that paid in the middle of the market as opposed to the highest since I knew those firms would challenge me and I would have a great opportunity to learn. Since I have gained a lot of experience, I feel like I am in a position to pursue a job that will meet both my goals, which are ones that challenge me along with the salary that is near the higher end of the scale."*

What things are most important for you with this position?

Why are they asking this question? The interviewer wants to know what your expectations are for the job so they can determine if you will be a good fit.

Think about some of the elements of the job that you are applying for and put that in your answer:

> *"I am able to work in various environments, but if I have to choose just a couple of aspects of this position, it would be an environment where I can continue to take on more responsibilities as I grow in my job and one that is team based where we can work together to meet objectives."*

What is Your Expected Salary?

This is a tricky yet important question. This question can influence the interview in a big way. The reason this question is asked is to see if the company can afford you before they take the time to convince you to work for them.

They could also be looking to see how you value your work. Do you have the confidence to ask them for the money you deserve, or are you willing to accept any offer they give? The salary questions will be asked in one of two ways; sometimes they ask both:

1. What are you currently making?

2. What do you want to make?

These questions can either be asked at the beginning or towards the end of your interview. Sometimes, it is a good thing when these questions come into the conversation because it indicates that they are interested in you. On the flip side, if you are not prepared, this could cause a misstep and cost you the job.

Before you go into the interview, it is imperative that you check out the going rate for the jobs in your field and location. You can find this information on sites like glassdoor.com. This should help you to find a reasonable salary.

Second, you need to push the salary question to as close to the end of the interview as possible. If you are asked early on for the salary expectations, you could reply with:

> "I am looking more to find a position that fits in with my interests and skills. I am confident that you will offer a salary that is competitive within the current market."

This shows them that you are confident of what you can do and that you respect yourself enough not to sell yourself short. You are also giving them the chance to earn your respect. This tactfully lets them know that you are not desperate. If they press further, you can reply with:

> "According to some research that I have performed and my experience, I understand that 75 to 90k per year is typically based on the requirements and role."

This frames the answer in a way that it gives them a straight, hardball answer. Instead, you have shown them that you have taken the time to do research and can work together to find an agreeable amount.

How Many Hours Do You Want to Work?

Much like the salary questions, this is one you have to be careful about regarding your answer. You do not want to come off as a slacker or a workaholic. It is best if you can avoid giving them an exact number—if at all possible. You never really know if the interviewer is looking to learn about your efficiency or your willingness to work a standard work week.

Before your interview, look at the culture of the company. If they clearly like people who work just the required number of hours, emphasize your time management and organizational skills. If they like people who work long hours, show them that you are flexible and have a willingness to work.

Let's take a look at a good answer to this question:

> *"I have always been great at creating and maintaining an efficient schedule that will let me work the same number of hours each week. Of course, if I have a particularly important project, I am fine with increasing my hours a bit to make sure I produce my best work."*

What is Your Availability?

Every job you apply for is going to ask you about your work availability, and it is important that you are honest about your commitments. If you know you have to take your kids to school in the morning, let them know.

If you are looking for a full-time position, make sure that you emphasize that you are willing and can put in a full work week and that you would be willing to put in the occasional overtime. If you are applying for a shift or part-time job, make sure you are clear on your flexibility and the hours you can work.

Here is a good answer for shift or part-time work:

> *"I have availability during school hours while my child is at school, from nine in the morning to three in the afternoon, Monday through Friday. I can also work most weekends, especially during the day."*

Please note that employers are not legally allowed to ask you if you have children, and you do not have to volunteer that information.

Here is a good answer if you are applying for a full-time job:

> *"I am available Monday through Friday, and I am flexible about the start and end time. I am also willing to take on some additional hours if need be."*

Was it You or Them?

In this group of questions, we will look at everything the interviewer might ask about your previous jobs. These questions let them see what kind of employee you are. It is important that you remember the dos and don'ts we talked about earlier in the book. No matter how much you hated your last job or your last supervisor, you should not let those emotions affect your answer. If you do, that is going to leave a bad impression, and you will come off as unprofessional.

You should also make sure you tell the truth. Remember: they can find out if you were lying. A simple phone call to your previous employer will let them know what happened.

Why Did You Leave Your Last Job?

Employers tend to be curious as to why you left your last job. They are looking to hire a person who is going to stick around for a while, so make sure you are prepared to explain why you left the previous jobs you held.

There is likely going to be a number of reasons why you left your job, so try to focus on the reason that shows you are a better fit for the new job than you were for your last job.

Some good reasons for leaving a position include looking for more responsibility, changing your career direction to focus on your passions, or moving to a new area or family reasons. These types of answer show that you have family, passion, or ambition ties to the location of where you are job hunting.

Some bad reasons for leaving a position include not liking your coworkers, being bored, or leaving because you wanted to make a change. These types of answers tell the employer that you might be someone who is hard to work with, cursed with a short attention span, or easily dissatisfied.

Let's take a look at a good answer for a person who has switched jobs several times and who is looking to get hired as a medical assistant. Some of the responsibilities for this could include assisting with patient exams, recording medical histories, and interviewing patients:

> *"Since high school, I have held three different jobs. While I was getting my associates degree, I worked as a part-time personal care assistant for a senior woman. While I enjoyed what I did, there was no chance of it becoming full time once I graduated, so I moved onto a full-time job. Next, I worked as an orderly. I loved getting to work with the medical staff and patients, but I was looking for more responsibility, so I took a job as a medical assistant. I worked in that position for two years and then my husband was transferred to Chicago. Therefore, I am looking to get a medical assistant job here. I love working as a medical assistant, and I am really excited to find a job where I can help the organization."*

This is a great answer because every job changed the person and brought them closer to the position they were interviewing for. It is easy for the employer to see that they are passionate about their career. The position they are seeking is a better fit for their needs and goals. This means that they are likely going to stick with this job for a long time.

What responsibilities did you have at your last job?

Why are they asking this question? The interviewer wants to know if what you are interviewing for is similar to another job or it will be a step up in responsibilities.

Think about the responsibilities you will have in the job you are interviewing for when you are describing your previous job. You need to show them you can handle the new job's responsibilities since you have already done the majority of them in your old one:

> *"From the way I understand this job, most of the responsibilities of my previous job would have been similar including..."*

Has your job affected your life?

Why are they asking this question? The interviewer wants to know how you balance your personal and professional life.

Give them examples that show you have a strong work ethic and an ability to balance your professional and personal life:

> *"Family life is my first priority, but I have to balance it around a job. If I am not doing my job and/or creating a financially sustainable lifestyle for my family and myself, then it is going to be hard for me to concentrate on anything. This is why I am looking for a new job that will let me be able to do this. I do not think of it as my job affecting my lifestyle but more about balancing the two. If my job makes me stay late at the office for a few days, then I will make opportunities to spend time with the family on the weekend or wake up earlier each morning."*

Why do you have a gap between (this date) and (this date)?

Why are they asking this question? The interviewer wants to know more about your work ethic and is worried about the gap in your employment. They want to know if you were fired, quit, and if so, why.

Even if the reason why there is a gap in employment was not your decision, frame it in a positive sense. Tell them of any mistakes you have learned from and the ways they have made you better:

> *"Unfortunately, I was let go because of downsizing. I enjoyed my year and a half at the company. It let me learn more about banking and helped me develop my skills. In the beginning, it was a bit rough managing my time effectively, but I improved greatly, and look forward to bringing my abilities to the next opportunity."*

What didn't you like about your previous job?

Why are they asking this question? Nothing will ever go as expected on a job. The employer wants to know how you will deal with it.

Give them a negative that could be applicable to a previous job but that you do not think would be a problem with the job you are applying for now. Explain how there might be some things that you disliked, but you could work successfully:

> *"I normally do not focus on the negatives of a job since I believe it is impossible to work in perfect conditions. Part of having a job is the ability to work in a collaborative environment. Management said to contact them whenever we finished an assignment instead of checking in with coworkers to see if they need help. Unfortunately, this slowed down our process and we were not able to help each other effectively."*

Which boss was the worst?

Why are they asking this question? Having conflicts with management happens and the interviewer is trying to understand how you might manage the problem.

You have to admit that you have problems working with a specific manager and why. Explain the way you dealt with the problem and the outcome:

> *"Well, I would not say that any of my bosses were the worst. It is normal for managers and the people that they manage to have a conflict now and then. There was one boss that I was concerned about because things with him started on the wrong foot. I had worked about two years on a job, and I got assigned to a new manager. The way he managed was much different from my other manager, and I had to learn how to adjust to it. I was used to a hands-on manager, and this new one was very hands off. Each one had different ways they wanted to communicate and report information. After some missteps with the new manager, I asked to speak with him so that we would clear things up and figure out what his expectations were. It was very helpful, and we ended up working together a lot better after that."*

Why did you quit your last job?

Why are they asking this question? The interviewer wants to know what caused you to quit a job. They want to know if it might or might not happen if you were to take this job.

Give them an explanation that focuses on the reasons why that particular situation was not working for you, what you learned from it, and why a new job would be better for you:

> *"I had been at my last job for four years. It was a great experience since I was about to be with a company while it grew from a team of four to 20 employees. I was offered an*

opportunity to train others and serve in a team leadership role. When the industry took a downturn, the team dwindled, and I no longer had an opportunity to use my new skills. I started interviewing for other positions before I left, but it got too hard to attend multiple follow-up interviews without it affecting my job. I decided to leave so I could concentrate completely on finding the next opportunity."

What is the most boring job you have ever had?

Why are they asking this question? The interviewer wants to know what environment is a good fit for you.

Try to focus on a job where the required skill set was completely different from the one you are interviewing for. Tell them how you maintained your professionalism and exceeded in spite of the job not being as fun as you thought it would be:

"The first job I had out of college was data entry all day, every day. I like being around people, and this job was very boring. In spite of finding the job boring, somebody had the confidence to give me an opportunity, and I took pride in my work and did my best. I ended up being the employee with the most accuracy and fastest speed."

Why have you held so many jobs?

Why are they asking this question? The interviewer wants to know how long you are going to remain with this job and is worried about your past.

Try to focus on why this job is a great fit for you and why you changed jobs so you could advance yourself:

"I have had to take risks to learn and advance myself in order to be in the position to compete for this job. Each opportunity was a great way for me to learn early in my

career. I am now looking for a solid opportunity that I can grow in."

What Are Your Reasons?

With this set of questions, the interviewer is looking to find out why you are interested in the job. This lets them know how much time and energy you are willing to invest in your role. A person who is applying for the job for the money is probably not going to work as hard as a person who is passionate about the position.

While there is nothing wrong with going after the job because it offers a decent salary, answering these questions with a simple, "The money is good," answer is not going to set you apart from the others. You have to explain why you want the job even if you will not be getting paid as much for the work you will be doing.

Why Are You Interested in the Position?

This question is used by interviewers to see how committed you are to the position. They are interested in hiring a person who is willing to stay in the position for many years so that they do not have to go back through the interview process again.

We will use the passion framework for this one, and we will use the position of an agency account manager. Some of the responsibilities for this job could include executing marketing programs, planning development projects, and managing relationships with clients:

"I have always loved building creative solutions to problems others see as challenging. When I was attending Western University for my bachelor in business management, I worked as a summer intern at a marketing agency and loved it. After I graduated, they hired me, and I have worked there for the past three years. While there, I have been promoted from assistant account coordinator to account manager. I would love to work for your company because I want my career to progress in an agency that encourages creativity and thinking. For example, I love the campaign you did for Top Performance Sports, especially the short-form videos you integrated for their soccer gear with the online store they created for it. I also have a friend who works here. She has mentioned the rapid-iteration approach and team-oriented culture. Your approach and culture fit well with my action-oriented and collaborative style. She has also told me that you have the best creative minds in the industry, so it is the perfect company for people who look to find creative solutions to otherwise challenging problems. This is the kind of environment I am looking to work in."

This is a great answer because the candidate lets the interviewer know that they have a passion for something that is at the heart of the position, which is creative solutions. If you are ever faced with this type of question, make sure that you explain how your experiences and passions align with the role that you are seeking.

What Would You Want to Get from this Job?

If you have taken the time to research the company, this should be one of the easiest questions that you will be asked. The interviewer is checking to see if you truly want the job that you are applying for. You need to answer the questions straight from the description.

We will look at an answer to the position of a tax accountant. Some of the responsibilities that this position could include are conducting tax regulation training programs, meeting with clients to talk about tax matters, and preparing tax returns:

> *"I love getting to train people. I am a resident expert on the software programs at my current firm that is used to prepare tax returns. I love getting to lead the training sessions for the software, and I want to get to do more of that. In my next job, I want to be able to apply my knowledge of state and federal tax returns and computer software to teach others how to be successful in their jobs. I want to improve the world of everybody in the department so that we will be a high-performance team. I hope this will include leading regular training programs that will go over software programs and tax regulations."*

While this looks like a very obvious answer given the job description, a hiring manager loves to get this answer. It would surprise you to know how often candidates will answer questions with unrelated, unrealistic, or vague answers. For example, when it comes to entry-level jobs, some people will say things like "I'd like to have a job where I can set my own hours," or "I want to get a promotion quickly."

When it comes to this question, the best answer is a simple paraphrasing of the job description. Also, it is important that you let the interviewer know you are interested in building and learning more skills. This lets them know you are motivated.

How to Sell Yourself

These questions tend to be some of the hardest questions to answer. Not only do you have to make yourself sound good, but you are answering questions that ultimately have to be answered by the hiring manager. These questions can cause a lot of stress, especially if you are not prepared for them.

Much like your strengths and weaknesses, these questions provide the interviewer with insight into who you really are and how you view yourself. While it may not seem like it would, these questions help them see how well you would work with others. A person who thinks very highly of themselves and answers these questions in a self-centered way probably would not work very well with other people. They are more likely to bump heads with their coworkers.

You do not have to let questions like these catch you off guard. In fact, it is best if they don't. No interviewer wants to hear you say "Um" for a minute while you try to figure out what they want to hear.

Why Should I Hire You?

"Why should I hire you?" is a very common question during a job interview. Do not ever give them a short answer like "I'll be a hard worker," or "I will do a great job." You want to set yourself apart from the other candidates and provide specific answers. Provide the interviewer with a clear example that shows you are the best fit for the position you are applying for.

We will look at an example answer for the position of an insights manager. The responsibilities for this job could include analyzing competitive markets and trends, recommending improvements to existing programs, and identifying business opportunities:

> *"I love when I get to find new ways to grow a business. I understand you are trying to find somebody who can study consumers to discover growth opportunities and research the marketplace trends. I have shown great skill in those areas while at One Shot Photography as an insights analyst. I discovered that we were losing share because our consumers were choosing the smaller studios. I researched the issue and found a segmentation strategy that provided us with a new marketing approach. I then designed and executed the new plan that gave us a new marketing message and social media campaign. This gave the company its first year of sales growth in more than four years. Since then, they have grown every year. If you hire me, I will bring along my passion for growing a business using my research skills."*

This answer does a great job regarding the candidate connecting what they are passionate about to the role that they want. For a job like this, the hiring manager is going to want a person who can demonstrate their ability to find ways that a business can grow, and this answer proves that this person can do that.

Why Are You the Best Candidate?

This question will get thrown in so that the hiring manager can see if you fully understand the role in which you are applying for. They want to see if you can create a connection between your skills and the position they need to fill.

This is much like the previous question, so you can still use the same strategy to answer it. We are going to look at an example of the position of a sales manager at a dealership. The responsibilities for this job could be motivating the team members to deliver results and manage sales reps:

"I know you are looking to create a high-performance sales team. That is what I have a passion for, so let me explain why I am the best candidate. The job I currently have has me managing four sales reps. When I first took over the role, the team was struggling to reach their sales goals. I talked with each member to figure out their best role, and restructured the responsibilities so that everything played into their strengths. I discovered that one of the team members did not have the skills needed, so I got him reassigned to a different role, and I hired a person that had the skill set needed. During the last two years, my team has become the highest ranked sales team in the department. I am looking to find a position that provides me with a bigger team and more chances to grow a company's sales. I should be hired because I have shown my ability to build a good sales team, and that is what I can do for you."

The person brings in teamwork, which is what a hiring manager loves. They have shown their ability to see talent in others and find the right people for their team. They also show that they have compassion by getting the person that was not a good fit reassigned instead of just firing them.

Now It's Your Turn

When an interview comes to an end, you can expect to be asked if you have any questions or anything else to ask. While you most likely want to say "No" and run away hoping you left a good impression, that is not what you should do.

Several different closing questions can be asked, and we will cover many of them. You can pick the framework for each question based on the other information in the book and what the question is looking to help the interviewer learn about you.

Is There Anything Else?

Sometimes the interviewer will conclude the interview by asking if there is anything else that they need to know about you. If they still are not quite sure about you, this gives them the opportunity to see if you can make a good case for yourself to sway them.

When it comes to questions like this, you want to focus on something that is positive. Do not share your travel restrictions, the hours you would prefer to work, or that you want an expense account. Instead, this question should be used as your chance to tell them your best story or to resolve unresolved issues from past questions.

We will look at an answer to the position of a cook. Some of the responsibilities for this job are preparing orders and checking the freshness of ingredients:

"I wanted to make sure that I mentioned a cooking competition that I won last year. My last employer entered me into the Town Hall BBQ Cook-off. I was supposed to represent the restaurant with a recipe straight from our menu. The morning of the cook-off, I spoke with our specialty produce supplier to get the best ingredients before anybody else was able to grab them—I like doing this for the restaurant, just so that we have the best ingredients on hand. I also made sure that my best assistant was with me, as well as our friendliest waitress so that we could always be cooking and providing good service to people who came by to try our BBQ. Finally, I made sure to pick out festive utensils, napkins, and bowls for serving. The presentation is just as important as the food, so I wanted to make sure our presentation was on point. As a result, our BBQ beat out 20 other restaurants and won the grand prize. The publicity brought in new customers, and our sales tripled during the next few months."

This answer gave the candidate the chance to tell their best story, which they had not been able to share. As you are getting ready for your interview, make sure you have around three or four stories that highlight your skills. When the interviewer asks you if there is anything else that you want to add, this is your time to shine with your best story.

Do You Have Any Questions for Me?

Most interviews will end with the employer asking if you have any questions. This gives you the chance to place the interviewer in the position of selling you the job. You should not ask any questions that pressure the interviewer into having to tell you why you shouldn't work for them, or what they do not like. This is going to make them think they shouldn't offer you the job.

You also should not ask about work hours, benefits, or salary. This can be covered once you have been offered the job.

You do, however, want to get them talking about why they like working for the company or why they feel you would be a good fit. Interviewers love to give out advice. Ask their advice for a person who could be joining the company. This will allow them to give you advice as if you are a new employee. This provides a subliminal effect of changing their perspective from evaluating your skills to viewing you as an incoming employee.

Here are some good questions that you could ask them when the interview has come to a close:

- "What is your favorite thing about working for this company?"

- "What are the most important characteristics when considering somebody for this position?"

- "What type of advice would you give a new employee coming into this position?"

Again, all of these questions give the interviewer a chance to let you know how great the company is. You want them to start selling. If they have to sell you on the company or job, they are going to see you as a more favorable person for the position.

Also, if you ask them for their advice, it is going to show them that you value them and their point of view. Plus, most people like getting to help those who are seeking advice. If the interview went well, they would be more inclined to offer you the job.

Conclusion

Thank you for making it through to the end of *Job Interview Prepare to Get Hired: Top 100 Common Questions and Winning Answers*. It should have been informative and provided you with all of the tools needed to achieve your goals whatever they may be.

Job interviews do not have to be hard. With the right preparation and practice, you can fly through an interview and come out feeling great. You have got the skills, knowledge, and accomplishments—now you just have to prove to the interviewer that you can do all of that. Don't let your nerves get the best of you. Remember the things you have read and look back over them whenever you need to. Do your research, and you will be great.

Finally, if you found this book useful in any way, a review on Amazon is always appreciated!

Part 2: Job Interview

Will These Mistakes Cost You The Job?

Introduction

It is a pretty safe bet that everybody, at some point, is going to have to face a job interview. Whether it's searching for your first job after graduation, looking for new opportunities, or heading back to work after taking some time off, you are going to have to go to an interview. The most important step in getting a job is the interview. You might get noticed with an amazing resume, but the impression you make during the interview is what will make sure that you get the job.

There is no such thing as being too prepared for an interview. This includes researching the company to rehearsing the answers you can give, to the interview where practice is extremely important. Whether you are experienced or not, interviews are one of the most nerve-racking things you will ever do, and they can prevent very qualified people from getting the job.

There are different parts of the interview process, and they are all just as important as the other. This includes the clothes you wear, the things you say, and what you do once it ends. This book is here to help answer all of the questions you may have when it comes to preparing for a job interview. Through studying the information in this book, you will gain the confidence that you need to make it through your interview process.

This book will take you through every part of the interview process; before, during, and after. It also provides you with some vital information concerning what employers want and why simple mistakes will cost you the job.

This book will walk you through the most common mistakes made when applying for a job. This could be resume mistakes or how you answer the questionnaire on the application. You want to make sure that you get the interview so you can shine.

Then we will look at mistakes made before you go into your interview. This means you have impressed them with your application, and you have received the call for an interview. Now comes the time for you to get ready for the actual interview. This will include how you dress and how you prepare for the interview.

Then we will walk through some of the common mistakes that are made during the interview. These are probably the most important things to prepare for. You will learn that talking badly about your previous employer, no matter how bad he or she was, is a huge no-no, among other things.

To wrap things up, we will look at examples of good and bad interviews so that you can start to see what you should and should not do. If you are experienced in interviews, you may start noticing things that you have been doing that has cost you the job that you wanted.

Lastly, to make sure that you are always prepared for a job interview, you will find a job interview checklist at the end of the book. This will help you make sure you have done everything possible to make the best first impression.

By following the tips and ideas found within these pages, you can improve your odds of landing your next job and impressing the interview panel. This book will help you to become a success.

What Do Employers Want?

One of the main things people want to find out before an interview is what an employer is looking for, or what they want. The natural and simple answer is: leaders who can work well as part of a team.

In 2016, the National Association of Colleges and Employers (NACE) released a survey on *Job Outlook* and over 80% of those who responded said that employers are looking for evidence of leadership skills on a person's resume. Almost all of these people are also looking for candidates who can work on a team.

Within the same survey, employers also said that a strong work ethic, problem-solving skills, and written communication skills are essential for a potential employee. Employers give more weight to verbal communication skills than they do quantitative or analytical skills.

While hiring managers do look at your academic major, GPA, and extracurricular activities, leadership roles can help you to stand out amongst the other candidates.

As Richard Branson said, *"Hiring the right people takes time, the right questions and a healthy dose of curiosity. What do you think is the most important factor when building your team? For us, it's personality."*

While in an interview, the interviewer wants to get to know you. Your resume has told them everything that they need to know about your job skills, work history, and education. You will have to answer questions based on this information, but to blow them away, you have to speak beyond what is on your resume.

Each company has its own 'approaching the interview' process. Some will ask everybody the same question while others have a more open approach, allowing the conversation to flow naturally. There are a few things, as an applicant, which you can do to make yourself stand out amongst the competition. These are the things that employers are looking to see:

Understand the Company

"Never hire someone who knows less than you do about what he's hired to do." – Malcolm Forbes

The interviewer is going to want to know that you are familiar with the company. Before you sent in your resume, you should have researched the company to find out what it is that they do, how it's structured, where it operates, and other bits of information. This information is helpful during the interview so that you can show them that you have the skills and knowledge needed for the job. They don't want to hear generic answers to their questions; instead, tailor your response to show them how you would handle their company's specific needs.

It's Yours to Lose

Since the interviewer is looking to hire somebody who has your skills, and the process of hiring people takes up their time and takes them away from their regular duties, they typically come into the interview wanting to offer you the job. What you have to make sure you don't do is provide them with a reason to change their minds.

Show Success

"If you think it's expensive to hire a professional, wait until you hire an amateur." – Red Adair

As long as you show the interviewer that you can work well with others, make sure you "toot your own horn". They want to know about your success, especially those that relate to the position you are interviewing for. To make your life easier, make sure you come prepared with a few stories about things you have achieved.

Are You Answering the Questions?

While getting ready for your interview is excellent, and you should spend some time studying the kinds of questions that might be answered when it comes to the interview, you have to listen. Listen to what they ask and answer those questions. You don't want to answer their question with a practiced answer that has nothing to do with what they asked.

Make sure that you listen to their complete questions and give them a natural response. If you allow yourself to jump ahead and start thinking about how you are going to answer while they are still talking, that is going to annoy them. Trust that you can find your own words. You want to be conversational. This is going to help you connect with them.

They Want to Like You

"Don't hire anyone you wouldn't want to run into in the hallway at three in the morning." – Tina Fey

Since they know you have the skills they need, and they want to hire you, what do they want to get from the interview? Honestly, they are looking to see if they like you and if you will fit well into their team. Once you have been hired, you are going to be a person that they see and talk to every day. It is important that they know you because they are going to be spending a lot of time with you.

If you come off cliché with your answers, you aren't going to impress them. If you try to make your answers too perfect, they aren't going to learn about who you are—this will probably also annoy them. Make sure you are friendly and personable. Be a conversationalist instead of stating rehearsed answers. Build rapport with them.

Body Language

Are you sitting up straight? Being relaxed is a good thing, but slouching is not. You should be sitting up straight, looking professional, but also natural. Also, take note of any fidgets or crazy body movements you may make. Things like clicking a pen, picking at your nails, or tapping your finger can distract your interviewer from what you are saying.

Make sure you also add a warm smile as you speak, but keep it natural. Having a wide crazy green is not going to help you get the job unless you are applying to be a smiley face. Also, just because you are nervous, don't think that is negative. Interviewers expect you to be a bit nervous. Try your best to practice a little beforehand, be yourself during, and make sure you make eye contact. Most likely, this is going to help you relax enough to be yourself, and that is all that you want.

Your Looks are Important

The way you look when you come into the interview does impact whether or not you get the job. If you are dressed too casual, you will likely come off unprofessional or not serious enough about the job. If the hiring manager or the company has specific issues with odd facial hair, visible tattoos, or multiple piercings, these could also cost you the position. If you appear flustered, sweaty, and nervous, they may think that you aren't up for the job.

Dress nicely; come in clothing that is just a touch nicer than what you would wear day-to-day on the job. Make sure that you show up a little earlier so that you can come in on time and be calm and confident.

Eye Contact

This is extremely important, and the one thing that job candidates find difficult. The interviewer wants you to look them in the eye when you speak, and when they ask questions. If your eyes are constantly looking around the room, you may come off as uneasy, bored, or lying. You don't want to come off seeming like you want a staring contest, but normal eye contact during the exchange can help to create a connection.

Are You Real?

Whether you have come up with the answers or are answering spontaneously or are telling them the real story or what you think they want to hear, the interviewer wants you to be 100% familiar with how well matched you are for the position. Use your truthful answers to create a picture of the best possible match. Too often, candidates only share the part of their story that they think the interviewer wants to hear. This causes you to come off sounding phony.

Understand Your Weaknesses

"Hire an attitude, not just experience and qualification." – Greg Savage

Interviewers don't want to hear things like, "My biggest weakness is that I work too hard." That's not a weakness, and nobody is perfect. Interviewers know this, and they want to find people who can learn from their shortcomings and have figured out how to work around them. Make sure you know how to talk about two or three real weaknesses, and how you can overcome them.

Self-Starter

While they want to make sure that you can work well with others, they also want to know that you aren't going to sit around and twiddle your thumbs, waiting to be told what to do. They will look for clues that you can work independently, while also respecting coworkers and the company's management structure.

Flexibility and Adaptability

Employers like to ask behavioral questions, where interviewers will ask how you handled certain situations in the past, to see how your abilities are when it comes to adapting to new situations with success and ease. If you have job stories that show you can quickly solve problems, you will show them that you are a person who can rise to the occasion.

Reasonable Expectations

Not only is the employer looking to see if you are going to be a good fit, but they also want to know that the job is a good fit for you. Having an unhappy employee is not going to help anybody, and the hiring manager isn't going to want to have to go through the hiring process soon after.

While the majority of employers want you to be interested in growing vertically and horizontally within the company, it is important that you show them you know what the position is and isn't. They want to know how quickly you expect to advance, and to make sure that expectation is reasonable.

Respect for Management

The hiring manager wants somebody that fits into the company and respects management, as well as the culture and mission of the company. If you answer with stories about how you are smarter than management and always save the day, you are not going to come across very well. Even if the management in your last position was terrible, always share stories in a way that makes you come off as capable and resourceful, while not putting others down.

High Maintenance Personality

"Hire character. Train skill." – Peter Schultz

Some candidates walk in with complaint written all over their face from not getting to bring their parents or having to wait too long. Or, they emailed and called every day leading up to the interview asking questions. These are not good signs.

During the interview, the way a person shares a story will show if they expect a lot from others, in a bad way, and view things from their point of view and nobody else's. The company wants somebody willing to pitch in and help when need be.

Problem Solver

"Recently, I was asked if I was going to fire an employee who made a mistake that cost the company $600,000. No, I replied, I just spent $600,000 training him. Why would I want somebody to hire his experience?" – Thomas John Watson Sr.

Managers love problem solvers. Of course, you want to show that you wait until you have gathered up all of the facts and make sure that there is a problem that needs solving. Some people come into an interview with plans on how to fix a business, positive that these ideas are going to help them get the job. Having stories about how you fixed problems in previous positions are a good thing. Going into the interview to try to fix a company that you don't work for is not good.

Don't Be Too Eager

While employers do like candidates who are enthusiastic about the position, you can end up coming off as too enthusiastic. Being too enthusiastic can make you appear overly needy, and this makes you look bad. This will lower your chances of being hired. For example, if you are currently working somewhere else and you tell them that you can start right away, this could hurt your chances of getting the job. This shows them that you are willing to make an unprofessional exit from your current job by leaving without notice. The interviewer will start questioning if you are the right person for their team.

While it is a good idea to send a thank you after you have an interview, following up too much can hurt your chances. Emailing or calling them several times to check in on the status will only cause you to come off as desperate and is going to get on their nerves.

Do You Have The Skills?

You should have checked out the job description long before your interview, and you should have found examples of the skills you have that match what they want. Some companies have individual tests or interviews to check for these things, so make sure you are ready. If there is something that they want that you haven't done in a while, make sure you brush up on it before the interview.

Ask Them Questions

"When you hire people that are smarter than you are, you prove that you are smarter than they are." – RH Grant

A job interview is not a one-way street. The interviewer wants to see that you are interested in learning about them. This shows that you care about what work you do and whom you work for, instead of taking anything you can get. Asking them questions ensures that the people, position, and company is a good fit for what you want for yourself.

Make sure you go into the interview with three to five questions ready to ask them when given a chance. Some questions that you can ask the interviewer are:

- What resources or staff support will I have to reach the department's goals?

- What are the main priorities this position needs to accomplish within the next six months?

- What is the culture like here?

- In the last year, what has been the position's biggest challenge?

- What caused this position to open?

These questions show the interviewer that you want to be successful, and they appreciate when you show this type of interest.

Why Mistakes Can Cost You the Job

Interviews are an important time to make sure you shine, but they are also important for the company. Making the wrong choice for an employee can bring devastating results. That is why a simple mistake can cost you the job. To help you understand why the interview process is so important, we are going to look at what it costs a company when they hire the wrong person.

The people that a company hires are the biggest factor when it comes to the success and growth that the company will experience. Employees are not only the people who deal with customers regularly, but they are also essential parts of the machine when it comes to providing needed services and delivering goods. When a business does not have a core team of effective and quality employees, it is impossible for them to stand apart, create a brand, and make their own customer experience.

During the hiring process, it isn't all about finding that person who can immediately fill the position—like a person who may not fit all of the requirements. It is important that they dedicate the resources and time needed to fill the position with someone who is dedicated to creating long-term success for the business. Employees are the most valuable and important asset to a company. Without employees, the business will cease to exist because no business is going to operate successfully and efficiently.

Everybody hired by a company brings along something unique, and it is important for employers to seek out people who have the best qualities. Not only do they end up wasting time not making the best decision during the hiring process, but they also lose a lot of financial resources on that bad fit.

According to some estimates, it can cost over a quarter of a million dollars to find and hire somebody. If they end up being the wrong person for the role, add to this the toll that the bad hire takes on their colleagues and managers, plus a whole host of other costs if they have to be replaced.

While most businesses know they need to make the best choice first, many of them do not use the resources they should, up front, to avoid this problem. A bad hire has a ripple effect among everybody within the business and the quality of the services.

Most businesses have, at some point, hired a person who ended up not being a good fit. There are many different things that HR can do to make sure that they don't waste their time recruiting, interviewing, and offering jobs to the wrong person.

The Cost of the Wrong Person

According to Jorgen Sundberg, CEO of Link Humans, the cost of recruiting, hiring, and training new hires can cost as much as $240,000. If that person turns out to be a bad fit, there are extra costs the business incurs, not the least of which is having to find their replacement. Brandon Hall Group discovered several variables that can play a part in coming up with the cost to replace bad hires. These include:

- Litigation fees
- Weakened employer brand

- Outplacement services

- Lost consumers

- Disruptions to projects that haven't been finished

- Negative impact on performance

- Training and relocation fees for replacements

- Staff time and advertisement fees for recruitment

The Effects of Bad Recruiting

When recruitment is done badly, there are many negative impacts that a business can suffer. Here are a few:

- *A bad candidate can reduce future job applications* – When there is a bad candidate experience, it can disillusion candidates. This disillusionment can cause a company to lose out on the opportunity to hire future people. 42% of people who responded to a CareerBuilder survey said that they decided never to seek employment from a company after a bad hire experience. 22% of people also said that they would not refer their colleagues or friends to the business either. It also causes the company to be less likely to get job applications from people who have read through the negative reviews on social media accounts by those disillusioned employees or candidates.

- *The added costs that are related to replacing the miss-hires* – These bad hires will either quit prematurely or be let go. Besides all of the obvious recruiting replacement costs or the costs that result from the hiring manager having to spend more time on recruiting instead of what their regular job is, the most significant revenue cost comes from not having any productivity in the role during the business day while it is vacant. If this vacant position is a revenue-generating position, the revenue you could have made during those vacant days can't be replaced. And even if it's not a revenue-generating position, the vacancy means that all of the other employees will be stressed more because they will have to do more work to fill in this gap. To make things worse, if recruiting ends up taking a long time to fill the position, the cost of this open place will increase dramatically.

• *Hiring a bad employee can reduce the power of the company's product brand* – At many businesses, it is hard to separate the employer brand and the product brand. For example, Google and Apple are one and two on product and employer brand. With this interconnection of the two, if the employer brand gets damaged, so does the product brand. So if the employer brand gets hurt by hiring a person with inexperience or due to a questionable hiring process, it can end up hurting the product brand and the sales it could create. These relationships between the brands are growing every day as social media sites, such as Glassdoor, continue to grow. It is straightforward for people and customers to learn about a negative employee or candidate experience, and then they use that to change their purchase decisions and job search. It's crazy, but any function that could indirectly hurt a company's product brand will guarantee a lower budget and a rough time in the corporation.

• *Lower productivity* – When a company has a weak employer brand, it will cause lower-quality hires in every job that gets filled. This is proven through the data from the Corporate Executive Board because they show that with a strong employer brand, the quality of your hires will increase by 9%. A weak recruiting process that constantly hires underqualified people is going to lower productivity, especially from the employee. For example, a bid hire works 10% below average, multiply the 10% by the average revenue per employee, and this will show the estimated cost of hiring just one person that works below average. If Apple were to hire one below average employee, it would cost them $240,000 in revenue.

• *Lowered revenue in positions that have a revenue impact* – When below average performers are hired in important revenue-generating and sales jobs, it can result in a huge reduction in revenue. There are also negative revenue impacts on several other revenue-impacted jobs, such as customer service and product development, as a result of bad performance due to below average hires in these roles. Bad hiring will cause less innovation when it comes to products and bad customer service once a sale has been made.

• *Lower product sales* – When there is a bad candidate experience, it frustrates and upsets other candidates. A large portion of these disillusioned candidates will strike back by not purchasing the company's retail products. Due to this disillusionment, it will cost the company product sales of 23% from candidates who, if they had a positive experience, would have been more likely to purchase services or products from them. It will also cost them sales from 9% of the candidate's friends and colleagues that they urge not to buy from the company. This means that it is crucial for the business to find out if the people they are interviewing are current customers and then to make sure that the company is responsive if they choose not to move forward with them.

Why Does This Still Happen?

If it is so time-consuming and expensive to hire the wrong person, why does this still happen?

CareerBuilder believes that one reason why companies hire the wrong person is that they rush to fill an open position. They performed a survey in 2012 asking why companies make bad hires; they discovered that 43% made a bad hire when they felt they had to pick somebody quickly.

This urgency can be created in many different ways. This includes: an important role in the company that needs urgent attention, a project might need a new talent, an important employee has suddenly left, or the current staff may be overextended. Hiring managers are often left feeling anxious about putting a person in a vacant spot that they often overlook the flaws of a candidate and end up hiring a person who does not meet the needs of the company.

22% of the respondents of the CareerBuilder survey felt that they lacked the skills necessary to hire and interview people. When it comes to hiring the wrong person, it shouldn't be the person hired that gets blamed; instead, it is the person who did the hiring that made the wrong choice. Hiring managers have to know what to look for during the hiring process.

What Is Needed to Hire the Right Person?

The first step in hiring the right person is making sure that the company has the right type of person leading the hiring process who is well informed of what the business needs. Talking with the executives and hiring manager about the needs of the business can help to make sure that a better decision is made.

This is why most companies have a standardized interview process. This provides them with the tools and questions to help them evaluate candidates. Peer-to-peer interviews and behavioral interviews help hiring managers to determine if a person would be a good fit for the company. This process works the same for every person that has applied for a job with the company. Those in charge of the hiring process are trained to spot any red flags during the interview process.

The process is meant to help people become relaxed before asking them questions that are worded in such a way that allows the interviewer to learn more about the person.

Almost a tenth of the survey respondents said that their bad hires did not work out because they didn't fully understand the company's culture or brand. This is why it is important for a company to make sure that they have a clear brand, and the prospective employee should do plenty of research to learn more about the company.

Common Mistakes Made When Applying for a Job

Before you get a job interview, you have to apply for the job. If this is not done successfully, then you will never get to shine for the hiring manager and convince them to hire you.

While the ultimate goal for everybody is to get a job, the way everybody approaches this will vary, and several questions exist when it comes to strategy. For example, are you going to browse through online listings or are you going to use a newspaper? Are you planning on calling up the people you know within a specific field to help you find some possible leads or are you going to try to find things on your own? How much of a role do social media sites, such as LinkedIn, going to play?

The hardest part of finding a job is figuring out what it is that you want to do. Having a degree in a particular field or working several years in a certain industry shouldn't limit all of your options. It isn't uncommon for a person to have five or more different careers during their life. It may come off as cliché, but every day of your life you will learn something new about your likes and dislikes and strengths and weaknesses.

When you are picking a career or changing one, there are two questions that you need to think about.

First, while a certain job or industry may look enticing, are you prepared to do what it requires day in and day out? You have to ask yourself whether you are going to want to meet all of the demands of the job or if you think it is something that is going to impress your friends.

Second, are you ready to live the life the job requires? For example, while being a personal assistant to a celebrity might sound like a dream job, are you willing to be at their beck and call all day? Are you going to be able to withstand belittling comments and a possible difficult personality? High-paying or high-profile jobs won't give you much in the way of free time. If you aren't familiar with the primary duties of a position, try to talk to somebody else that is in the field or a career counselor so that you can learn as much as possible. You need to do a lot of research into the job, what it requires, and the company before ever accepting it. What you think might be a dream job could end up being a nightmare.

Career planning is a science all on its own, and you shouldn't feel weird to ask for help from professionals when it comes to figuring out where to go next. If you are still in college, there are probably plenty of these professionals in your school's career planning office. If you are familiar with the workforce, there are many career planning centers in your community. Do some research and set up an appointment to meet with one. Some career planners do work virtually, which will allow you to connect with planners that aren't in your area.

Career Tests

If you are not sure what you want to do, career tests are an excellent way for you to learn more about your career possibilities and preferences. Most tests are available through trade and industry associations and most commonly available online. Many of these associations publish magazines that will provide you with insights into a particular career. It might be a good idea to take some time to investigate a job more.

If you do not have the time to meet up with a career professional, there are online sites that can help you research types of careers that could work for you. Some people thing career tests are stupid or a waste of time, but they can be helpful. Since it is true that a career professional, pre-manufactured form, or computer doesn't know you better than you know you, you shouldn't solely rely on what these things tell you. However, try to keep an open mind; if there is something the test says might be a good idea that you have never thought about, take a few minutes to read up on it. You never know; it might be your dream career.

Employers will also sometimes use career tests as part of the screening process, and it can be helpful if you are already familiar with some of the most common tests used. These include:

- CAPS – Career Ability Placement Test

CAPS is a timed test. It may not tell you whether the answers were right or wrong, but it does give you an indication of how you scored in eight areas of language usage, verbal reasoning, spatial relations, and mechanical reasoning.

- MBTI – Myers Brigs Type Indicator

Using the MBTI has started to become popular in figuring out if a candidate will fit into a company's culture. MBTI measures a person's personality in four areas: judging/perceiving, sensing/intuitive, thinking/feeling, and extrovert/introvert.

- SII – Strong Interest Inventory

The SII measures a person's interests based on their answers about different activities that fall into six categories: realistic, enterprising, artistic, conventional, investigative, and social. The SDS, or Self-Directed Search, is similar to SII. It focuses on the same areas, but it is a shorter test.

Recruiters and Counselors

Recruiters and counselors have become very popular among job seekers over the past few years. With the increasing number of applicants, it has made effective and experienced counselors important brokers of employers and positions. Recruiters and counselors are not only able to help a person save time by working through the process of sifting through jobs and applicants, but they can also offer professional advice to applicants so that they can find what it is that they are looking for and help them sell themselves more effectively.

Now, you may be wondering what the difference is between a recruiter and counselor. You know those advertisements on web pages? Those were put there by recruiters. These recruiters could be an employee of the company that is looking to hire somebody, or they are a third party that has been contracted by the company. If it is the latter, then there was probably a fee involved—but that is typically paid for by the company looking to hire.

If you head to a career coach or counselor, you will handle any costs that are required, unless it is an outplacement service that your former employer or college is offering. Career counselors do not help you find a job; instead, they help you figure out the type of job you need to look for. If the job market confuses you, a career counselor is there to help you to clarify your career goals and aim you in the best direction. You have to watch out for the type of contract you sign. Some counselors insist on being paid first, and their fees can be as high as $2,000 to $15,000. You want to find a counselor who has Master Career Counselor credentials, state licensure, and charges by the hour. A great way to find a counselor is to check out ncda.org.

The following are some helpful tips when it comes to working with counselors and recruiters:

- Respond to any inquiries made by counselors or recruiters if they reach out to you, even if you have no interest in the position. This will put you on their radar, and you want to be there to make a good impression because there could be another position that opens up in the future that you do want.

• Keep in touch with them to build rapport and stay in their mind when new jobs come up.

• Be upfront about your job goals and expectations. This includes the things you are interested in and what you aren't.

• Don't double dip. If you have already been in contact with one recruiter for a certain position and then another one gets in touch with you, be truthful with them about your other relationship.

• Feel free to let counselors and recruiters know that you want what you talk about and all your information to remain confidential. While most of them automatically work this way, it is best to say something to make sure that you are both on the same page.

Techniques for Job Seeking

There are many different ways to try to find a job. Some of them include:

• Sending out resumes to employers that are unsolicited, also referred to as the direct contact method.

• Calling a personal contact, also known as networking. You can ask other professionals how they ended up getting their current position, and there are going to be some that say they got their job through a business contact, family member, or friend. No matter what your profession is, the chances are that you probably know somebody in that field already or at least somebody who knows somebody. Either way, you should be able to locate somebody in the field who can help you out. Even if they aren't able to offer you a job, they may be able to aim you in the right direction. Making connections are a great way to get into a new career field and advance your career.

If you haven't been able to locate somebody who can help, there are many other ways to make contacts. Try to find local organizations that specialize in what you do and make a point of attending their meetings. You can also contact your college's alumni association and see if you can find another graduate who is in that field. You can also go online and engage with some other professionals on job boards. While you may not get offers right away, don't be surprised if you end up hearing from some of these contacts later on about new opportunities.

• Getting help from an employment service firm or recruiter. If you have no time to pore through the classifieds, actively look through job postings, or print up a resume and cover letters, employment services can help. Whether you want a direct-hire job or a temporary job, there are plenty of staffing firms to help service what the job seeker needs, whether executive or entry-level.

But what exactly do they do? They do whatever it is that you want them to do. They can be specialized in what they do, or general. They may offer one specific service that helps a small group of job seekers, or they may provide a large number of services to help a large number of people.

If you want to have a staffing firm help you out, don't pick one blindly. The National Association of Personnel Services and the American Staffing Association are two great choices that will uphold ethical business practices. They do require a membership though.

• Answering a help-wanted advertisement. While seeing the words "Help Wanted" probably makes you think of the classified pages in a newspaper, that is by no means the only place to find help-wanted ads. With technology, there are now literally thousands of websites that are for job hunters. You can access millions of job openings from around the world with just a couple of clicks. Professional and trade organizations are a perfect place for information about profession-specific jobs. Magazines are a great place to look for job listings, which can also be accessed online.

Resume Mistakes

Now you have gone through the process of trying to find a job to apply to, the next thing you have to do is get an interview by creating an attention-grabbing resume.

Your resume is what employers read to get to know your skills and decide if they want to spend the time and energy to bring you in for an interview. This is why you have to make sure that your resume has as much detail and information as possible, without going beyond the one-page limit. Another function of the resume is to be attractive and draw as much attention your way as possible. The only way to get a job offer is to get noticed. Very few people still send out hard copy resumes through the US mail. Instead, this process is being replaced by online recruitment techniques, which will sometimes give you the chance to attach a file. In some other cases, you will have to fill out online forms that are going to be different depending on the position and company.

- Unsolicited Resumes

A huge frustration that job seekers have to face is looking through a company's open positions and not finding a spot that works for them. What should happen if your dream company isn't hiring people? Send them your resume anyway!

Most people think about sending their resume to human resources, but you should think beyond HR. Get in touch with line managers. They are the ones who usually make the hiring decisions. See if you can get the name of a person in the department that you would like to work in. At best, try to start a dialogue so that you can get a good idea as to what they want. At worst, they will push you back towards HR.

There are also many companies who will provide you with a chance to sign up for notifications about job openings in your area of interest. You can also do this through recruitment websites like Monster. The resume is what stands between you and an interview. Most jobs are going to try to hire within first before posting a job opening—this saves them time and money. However, if they are unable to find somebody within the company to fill the position, and they already have your resume, you may be getting a call. That being said, if you have a bad resume, it will likely see the trashcan.

Let's take a look at some of the worst resume mistakes so that you can make sure to avoid them:

1. Grammatical errors and typos

This may be the most obvious thing, but your resume needs to be grammatically perfect. If it's not, the employer is going to reach some unflattering conclusions about you, such as "They don't care," or "They can't write."

2. Lacks specifics

The resume shouldn't have the obvious written on it. Employers want to understand the things that you have accomplished. Things like:

"I worked with employees in a restaurant."

"I recruited, hired, trained, and managed over twenty employees in a restaurant that made $2 million in sales annually."

These phrases can describe the same person, but the second one grabs your attention with its specifics.

3. Using the one-size-fits-all resume

When you try to come up with a generic resume to send out to every ad you see, you can almost guarantee that they are going to throw it in the trash. With the lack of effort, you come off like, "I'm not interested in the job. Frankly, any job is fine."

Employers need to feel special, and they want to receive a resume that has been made especially for them. They want you to clearly state how and why you will fit into their open position and organization.

4. Showing duties and not accomplishments

You want your resume to show how good you are at what you can do, but it's really easy to fall into the trap of listing your duties. Things like: updated files, worked with children, or recorded minutes at meetings are boring.

That reiterates the job description. Employers are more interested in the things that you accomplished than the things you did. Add more details so that you have something like this:

"Reorganized ten years of files to make them easily accessible to the department."

"Created three activities for preschool children and helped them create a ten-minute holiday program."

"Recorded weekly meeting minutes and create a Microsoft Word file for future reference."

5. Cutting things short or going on

Despite some of the things that you may have heard, there aren't any actual rules for the length of the resume. Why? Because people who have different expectations and preferences when it comes to resumes are going to be reading it.

This doesn't mean that you can send out five-page resumes. Generally speaking, if you can't say it in one, don't go over two. One is the best though. However, make sure that you don't cut too much good stuff out of your resume to try to get it to fit into a one-page standard.

6. Bad summary

Employers will read over your career summary, but they will often look over information that is fluff. Give them specifics and information that focuses on what they need.

7. No action verbs

Don't say things like, "I was responsible for…" Instead, add in some action verbs. These words show your initiative and punch up the tone of the resume. Try, "I developed a new onboarding program for new hires."

8. Left off important info

You might find yourself tempted to leave out jobs that you took to earn money for school. However, the soft skills that you learned throughout these jobs are more important than you might think.

9. Too much going on

If you have used a bunch of different fonts on your resume, it is going to give the person reading it a headache. Ask some friends to look at your resume to see if you have too much going on. If it's hard on their eyes, then you should probably redesign it.

10. Bad contact info

You could have the best resume in the world, but if the person can't contact you, then you won't be getting an interview. They aren't going to go out of their way to get the correct email or phone number. Double-check your contact information and make sure everything is correct.

Cover Letter Mistakes

The next thing employers are going to look at is your cover letter. These do not necessarily help you in the initial selection process; they can help make you stand out from the competition in later rounds. When responding to a classified advertisement, make sure that you use some of the keywords that the ad used.

Make sure you take the time to put together a letter for each application you send in. Like the resume, they want to know it is meant for them and not some generic cover letter that you make a couple of address changes to. Also, before going further into cover letter mistakes, make sure it is grammatically correct.

1. Focusing too much on you

Companies hire people to do things for them. This means that they would like to learn what you can do for them. While you should touch on your accomplishments, make sure you also explain why you can fill the void in their company.

2. Sharing information from every job you've ever had

Depending on how many jobs you've had, this could mean a very confusing and crowded cover letter. Instead of sharing about every job you've had, share what experiences relate to the position. Create a cover letter that talks about those skills instead of giving them your life story.

3. Sharing something uncomfortable

You don't want to share recent struggles you have faced in your cover letter. The person reading it isn't interested in why you were fired or laid off. This is going to be seen as a red flag. These things can be addressed in the interview if need be.

4. Writing a novel

Cover letters rarely get read, but have a novel-like cover letter is going to annoy many hiring managers. The majority of hiring managers prefer cover letters to be half a page or less.

5. Rehashing the resume

They already know your resume; they read that first. They aren't going to want to read back through it when it comes to your cover letter.

6. Being trite

Be specific in the things you can provide to their company. Avoid statements like, "I believe I am the best fit…"

Claiming Skills You Don't Have or Lying

As you may have noticed, lying wasn't mentioned in the last two sections. That was because it gets to have its own section because it is probably the worst thing that you can do when applying for a job. It's also something that you will see more of later in the book.

While you may feel tempted to embellish your application to increase your chances of getting an interview, doing so is a huge risk. Many consequences come with these lies.

There are several types of lies that a person can make on their resume or application. It can be a slight embellishment of the truth to extreme lies. Dates might be changed a bit to try and add gaps in employment. Achievements might be embellished a bit. There can be an overinflation of skill. Some people have even claimed work experience or degrees that they have never possessed. When it comes to legal issues of these lies, a company looks to see if it was "material" or not. This means if it could potentially influence a person's decision.

If you pay attention to the application process, there will probably be a disclaimer that says the information is needed to help assess a person's qualifications for a position. It continues by saying that if a person knowingly lies about this information, it is grounds for termination. If the application doesn't say this, most employers will still use their rights to fire a now-employee for omissions or lies during the application process.

Most states have at-will employment laws. All this means is that a person can leave their job whenever they want. It also implies that their employer has the right to terminate their employment relationship whenever they want unless their reason is illegal. If you get fired for lying on an application, it can cause a never-ending cycle. That means you have to tell the truth about them firing you for your next job application or you will risk omitting information, again.

When you lie during the application process, you also run the risk of losing your right to sue the employer if you have any legal claims, such as termination due to racial discrimination. That is what is known as the "after-acquired evidence" rule. It means that they can use whatever evidence they learned about you in defense against your legal claim. Their position is that if you had told the truth on the application, they wouldn't have hired you in the first place. They will have to prove your lies, how they were linked to your position and were enough for them not to have hired you.

If you are a licensed professional, lying during the job application can cost you your license.

It is not likely that you will face criminal charges for lying on the application, but some circumstances could cause criminal charges. For example, if you lie about military service to get some form of benefit, you can be prosecuted through the Stolen Valor Act. If you are applying for a federal or state job, you will probably face charges because you will have lied to a state or federal government agent.

Most white lies aren't going to cause a fraud charge, but fraud charges can be brought against you if the effect of the lie caused damage to the financial welfare of a business or a person.

You could also face civil liabilities. For example, if an architect lied about their credentials, they could be civilly liable for misrepresentation or civil fraud if a part of a building collapsed and hurt somebody.

The problems list is endless when it comes to not telling the truth on a job application. Plus, it sticks with you. It can make getting another job virtually impossible.

Not Being Creative or Unique

After you have taken the time to create your resume, it would be nice to think that you are all done. You have made sure that there aren't any spelling errors, it's not busy, and you feel ready to send it out.

The problem is: HR doesn't want to receive the same resume from everybody. They do not want to see a Word document template; they want something unique and creative.

The good news is that you don't have to write a new resume or cover letter for every single application. You can create a master copy of both with all of your certifications, skills, and experiences. Then, you can go in and make small changes to them for each job you are applying for so that they are all unique.

Now, there are some instances where changing your resume and cover letter completely will boost your chances of getting an interview. One instance will be if you have a job listing that you are extremely excited about. Go the extra mile with these. Customize your resume to show the types of things that the employer wants to see.

Another instance will be if you are making a career more. If you have worked as a sales representative for a while, and you want to change to an account manager, you are going to need to change your resume to show how the skills you have would work in the new position.

Yes, this might slow down your job application process, but once you get the hang of things, it will become easier. Plus, you will likely receive more interview calls.

Not Being True to Yourself and Your Skills

Employers need to know you, and you need to know that you are going to like the job. That is why it is so important that you make sure you are true to yourself and your skills.

Applying for a job that you are overqualified for is going to send off warning signs with the employer. Before we talk about that, let's talk about what it means for you. Are you going to be happy working 40 hours a week at a job where you will be doing things that are likely very easy for you to accomplish? Sure, it might easily work, but are you not going to get bored and tired of doing things that you could do in your sleep?

Now, as far as the employer is concerned, you could come off as desperate or unconfident. They are either going to think that you are in such a desperate need of a job that you are willing to take anything, or you are unsure of yourself and your skills. Either way, it is not going to make them want to hire you. They want somebody who is going to enjoy coming into work every day and who is completely confident in their abilities.

On the flip side of things, if you apply for a job that you are underqualified for, it is going to send off similar red flags for the employer. This is going to make you appear arrogant. It could also make them think that you are not paying attention, or just browsing through the job board applying to every job you see and not paying attention to what each one requires.

When you are applying for a job, you have to make sure that you are qualified for the job and would be happy doing the work. Employers want people who know themselves, who know what makes them happy, and what they want to do. They do not want to spend a ton of time training them in something they don't know anything about or worrying that they are going to quit because the work isn't challenging enough.

Show them that you know yourself.

Common Mistakes Before the Interview

You got your resume ready and a perfect cover letter. Companies are looking for someone who has experience, skills, and can fit into the company culture. They want to see if your ideas and personality will complement the people you will be working with. There are many ways you can let the interviewer know that you are the person.

Preparation

Getting ready for an interview takes patience and time. It is not something you can do ten minutes before you leave for your interview. It is something that you can learn, and it gets easier each time you do it. You start learning what questions will be asked and can figure out what answers will work best. The more interviews you have, the closer you will be to getting that perfect job.

The part that takes the most time is researching your prospective employer. It is also the most important part. The best way to show you are the best candidate is leaving a positive impression with the interviewer. The best way to do this is by knowing all the aspects of the company. You shouldn't do this early in the job search. You need to wait until you have been asked to come in for an interview.

- Finding the information

There are many tools and ways you can find the information you need. The first one is fairly obvious: knowing someone inside the company. If you don't know anyone, you might be able to create a contact. You might have a relative or friend that knows somebody that works at the company and can help you out.

You also need to find information about the company's competitors. There is a whole lot of information at local libraries, in magazines, newspapers, and journals. Focus on stats. Focus on companies who are in the same field as the one you are interviewing with. Take a close look at the ones who are leading the field. A few facts about them can help you during the interview.

Look for everything. Find enough information to be able to do a ten-minute presentation. Find as many facts as possible so you can talk intelligently about the company. You have to know what kind of services and products they offer, the customers they deal with, the business and name of their parent company, and businesses and names of any subsidiaries. Find out where they rank in the industry, profit and sales trends, type of ownership, size, and whatever else seems important to you. Learn the company jargon. If you know who will be conducting the interview, do some research on them too.

- Doing internet research

There are many places online where you can find information effectively and quickly. The first place to begin is the company's website. In addition to fundamental information, you need to find their history, mission statement, list of executives, and annual reports. If they have press releases, read the latest one. This shows the interviewer you know what is happening in the company. Many sites will give you facts you should know about an industry.

- Getting the most out of research

  o Look for online discussions where employees or experts discuss the company. This type of commentary may give you insight into the value and culture of the company.

o Read news reports and releases about what the company is feeling. Reports are more objective and give insight into how executives manage. Looking into third-party sources might give you insight into troubling information about the financial health of the company that might help you stay away from a sinking ship.

o Try not to restrict your search to just the newest listings. Some older postings might not have been filled and might have less competition since many job searchers only focus on the newest postings.

o Use the company's website to learn about certain careers. This information is probably being used by many companies and might be more general than more specific requirements that most companies look for. This can help you get an understanding of the career you are interested in.

o Use social media opportunities. Contacts on Facebook and LinkedIn might work for companies you are connected to. Find employees within your online network. Get in touch with them to get the information you need about the company.

- Mock Interviews

Sit down with some good friends that you trust and have some mock interviews. Have them ask you questions and see how well you can answer them. Ask for their honest feedback. Did you sound confident and assured? Were your answers off the mark or rambling? Would they hire the person that answered the questions? If not, then you need to do some work.

Have them record the interview so you can look at yourself through the eyes of the interviewer. Watch your body language since it tells you a lot about yourself. Were you slouching? Were you attentive and sitting up straight? Did you keep eye contact without staring? Your body language needs to show the interviewer that you are focused and alert. Do not cross your legs or fold your arms. Your hands can work against you as well. If you gesture when you talk, you need to get that under control. Keep your hands folded in your lap. If you take the time to work on all the above, you will be well on your way to a great interview.

- Phone Screen

Some companies will do a phone interview before they bring you in for an in-person interview. At this point, they already know that you meet all of their basic requirements. This pre-interview is simply their way of determining if you are worth their time to set up an in-person interview or continue with the process.

To be honest, phone interviews are not great because most people are never prepared for them, and people will often do a bad job of putting their best foot forward. Most of the time, it is because they don't give credit to how important the phone interview is.

There are three main reasons why companies will choose to do a phone interview:

1. They want to learn that you can perform certain tasks. They are looking for you to validate what you said that you could do. This is where you want to jump ahead of the competition by talking about your accomplishments and work experience. Then you want to take things a step further by providing them with a vision of what you can help them do.

2. They want to find out that you want the position. Nobody is interested in wasting their time interviewing somebody

who isn't interested in the job. You need to show them that you are passionate about your line of work.

3. They want to find out if they like you. You can have some of the best experience, and it could mean nothing to them if they don't think that you would be a great leader and a good team player. There have been plenty of hiring authorities who have chosen to "pass" on a candidate who had amazing qualifications. They pass on doing an in-person interview because they didn't want to waste their time meeting somebody who has a bad personality and poor leadership skills.

When getting ready for your phone interview, make sure that you have your resume with you. Most people think that this isn't necessary because the interviewer already knows their work history. No! Have your resume with you.

It is a known fact that during phone interviews—no matter how experienced the person is—the interviewee will get nervous or distracted and end up forgetting some of the most basic facts—like the correct name of an employer, detailed job descriptions, exact job titles, employment dates, and more. Plus, they will sometimes forget to ask their interviewer some important questions because they didn't have them written down in front of them. Here are some things you should make sure you do during a phone interview:

1. If possible, stand while talking with them. You can project your voice better, and this will make the conversation more engaging.

2. As stated earlier, have your questions and resume with you.

3. Ask what stage they are at in the interview process, and try to find out what was lacking from the other applicants that they have talked to. This shows that you have great leadership skills. This will give you a way to place yourself

ahead of the competition, and it will also engage the interviewer more, so you have a conversation with them instead of an interview.

4. You need to help the interviewer paint an accurate picture of you. Let your personality come through. Ask questions, laugh, be engaging. They have no clue who you are, and they are trying to create a picture of you as best they can without having to meet you in person.

5. If you are very interested in the job, invite yourself for an in-person interview once the phone interview has come to an end.

Let's take a look at how to invite yourself to an in-person interview. It may sound daunting, but it is very easy to do. This works because the interviewer will either validate their interest and set up another meeting or will be forced to tell you why they aren't interested in going forward with you at this time. Either way, you will know where you are on their radar and won't be left wondering.

As the phone interview comes to an end, once you have thanked them for the call, say, "I am very much interested in the job. I feel that my qualifications fit your needs, and I would like to get to meet with you for an in-person interview." Then, stop talking. Wait for them to respond.

They will either comply and set up an in-person interview or will say something along the lines of, "We are still in the process of screening other applicants. We will get in contact with you if we are interested."

If they show that they aren't interested, you may want to say something like, "Are you concerned about my qualifications?" This might get you a direct and honest answer, or not—but it's not going to hurt anything to ask. However, only ask this if it is apparent that they are concerned about your abilities to perform the job well; otherwise, this could end up doing more harm than good.

In the end, phone interviews are critical. They are somewhat more important than the in-person interview because if things do not go well, you won't get the in-person interview.

What to Bring

When it comes to an interview, they are about 80% preparation and 20% execution. We've already talked about different ways to prepare for your interview by using mock interviews and other practice tips. Now, let's look at how to make sure that you have everything that you need for your interview.

Let's take a moment to picture a scenario. You step into the office of your dream job, shake the hiring manager's hand, sit down, and then realize you have forgotten everything at home. You have no copies of your resume, no paper or pen to take notes with—it's a miracle that you put on deodorant.

Unfortunately, this lack of prep can end up costing you the job. To make sure that this doesn't happen, you should start preparing for the interview as soon as the interview has been set up.

Here are some things that you have to make sure you bring with you when you go to your interview, so you're 100% prepared:

1. Folder

You will no doubt have paperwork for the interview, so a folder is a great place to store all of these documents. This will show that you are organized. This is a soft skill that many employers are looking for.

2. Copies of your resume

Yes, you should have more than one copy of your resume with you. The chances are that you had already sent in a copy of your resume when you applied, but don't assume that the interviewer will have the copy on hand. They are busy people, so they may have forgotten to print it to bring with them.

Why do you need more than one copy? You don't know how many people will be on the interview panel, and more likely than not, all of them will want to see a copy of your resume.

3. Business cards

While your resume should have all of your contact information on it, and the business card might seem a bit old school, it doesn't hurt to have them with you. They are small and easy to carry, and you never know if somebody might ask for you. That's why it is always good to have some handy.

4. Work samples or portfolio

If you work in a creative industry, such as fashion, architecture, design, journalism, or advertising, make sure to bring plenty of the work you have done in the past. You should offer to send them an electronic copy of your portfolio later on. Depending on your line of work, you might want to bring along a sheet that shows all of the positive feedback that you have received from previous clients.

5. References

When your interview goes well—because after all of this it will—and they ask you for your references on the spot, make sure that you have a list prepared with all of the referees' contact information. Theoretically, you should be able to email the company your reference information once you get home, but this is a wrong approach. You want the company to have everything that they need to move forward with the hiring process. Plus, it will make you look more efficient if you have come prepared.

6. Pen and paper

Taking notes during your interview can be helpful for many reasons. First, it shows that you are actively listening and engaged in the conversation, and it ensures that you won't end up forgetting important information about the job. Plus, you can refer back to these notes later on in order to send out a personalized thank you note.

Before you start taking notes, make sure you ask the interviewer if it is okay that you do so. Make sure that you don't take so many brief records that you are unable to make eye contact. Also, bring more than one pen in case one runs out of ink.

7. Questions

To show that you are genuinely interested in the position, you need to make sure that you have prepared some questions to ask them in advance that shows you understand the company's culture, challenges, and core values. The following are a few questions that you could ask:

- How do your managers provide feedback to the employees?

- What is done to help encourage collaboration and camaraderie among coworkers?

- What are the most important things that I could accomplish during my first 60 days on the job?

- How are successes defined and measured?

8. Talking points

Job interviews are stressful and nerve-wracking. One of the best ways to reduce stress before you go into the interview and to help build your confidence is to make sure that you can jog your memory by taking a look at some notes that you jotted down before the interview that you want to make sure were covered. These could be notes about things like anecdotes that highlight your strengths and accomplishments and other specific skills.

You can come up with a list, which is a summary of the accomplishments you have achieved that are organized by skill sets, that you can look at right before you go into your interview. You should make sure that these accomplishments match up with the job's responsibilities. For example, if your interview is for a management position, you will want to talk about the last project you oversaw and describe how the project succeeded.

9. Identification

This may seem like a no-brainer, but it still has to be mentioned. You might have to have photo ID to get into the building, so check with the hiring manager before the interview to find out what their security requirements are. You would hate for security to ask for ID and not have it with you. They also may ask you for the company's name you are visiting, the name of the person you're meeting with, and the floor that the meeting is on. Make sure that you confirm all of this information when the interview is set up to make sure that you are not left confused in the lobby before the interview.

10. Contact information and directions

You should make sure a day before the interview that you know where you are going. Still, on the day of, make sure that you have the address written down should you need to use your GPS. Also, make sure that you have the contact information for the company should you need to get in touch with them beforehand in case anything goes wrong.

11. Mint

While you don't want to be chewing gum during the interview, eating a piece beforehand might be a good idea to make sure that your breath is fresh. Alternatively, you can pop a breath mint right before you head in for the interview.

12. A smile

Most of the time, a smile might come off as corny, but smiling will make you look better to the interviewer. Employers want to know that you are excited and enthusiastic about the job.

There are some things that you shouldn't bring to the interview as well. Here are a few:

- Your parents—as strange as it seems, it happens

- Excessive jewelry

- Drinks

- Food

- Chewing gum

When you have all of the things gathered and ready to go for your interview, you can move on to the next step in the preparation process.

Dress Code

This sounds superficial, but people judge you by the way you dress. However, that doesn't mean you have to wear Prada. What you look like on the outside shows what you are on the inside. If the interviewer can see that you took the time to pick the right clothing, it tells them that you put the same amount into your work. If you go to your interview dressed too casually, you are telling the interviewer that you don't care about the company or job. Dress up a bit more than you usually would if you were going to work for the day. You should take into consideration the basic rules listed below:

- Men

If you are interviewing for a professional position, always wear a suit. Wearing a shirt and tie might be fine for your current job, but it won't cut it for an interview. Wear conservatives colors, such as charcoal gray, navy blue, or black. Flashy or bright colors will distract the interviewer, and they won't listen to you as closely.

You can easily jazz up a conservative suit by changing up the shirt or tie or even both. If you have one suit, changing these can help a lot if you are interviewing with companies that require more than one interview on different occasions. Stay away from shiny shirts too—they should only be worn in nightclubs. Make sure you wear socks that blend in with your pants and shoes.

- Women

The proper attire for women in the workplace has changed much over the past few decades. The power suit that used to rule the scene has been downgraded to a pantsuit that doesn't look much different than a man's. Women wearing pants is now more acceptable and might be more appropriate in jobs where you will be walking a lot or getting in and out of cars. If you wear a skirt, the length of the skirt should be professional and tasteful. Nothing shorter than knee length is appropriate. It doesn't matter what the company's dress code is; women are expected to wear a suit to the interview.

The colors need to be conservative. Navy blue or black pants or a skirt along with a jacket would be your best choice. Stay away from colors such as powder-blue or pink— they don't help you look professional. Never wear anything that dangles—this applies to necklaces, bracelets, and earrings. Lastly, stay away from clothing that fits too tight—you won't be comfortable, and the interviewer won't take you seriously.

- Grooming

Personal grooming is critical, and you have to take care of it before you head out the door. Careful grooming shows self-confidence and thoroughness. Women shouldn't wear too much makeup or jewelry. If you paint your fingernails, make sure it is a conservative color.

Men need to make sure their facial hair is trimmed and neat. If you have a mustache or beard, it needs to be well groomed. If not, make sure you're clean-shaven at the time of the interview. If you have an interview at four but your five o'clock shadow shows up at three, make sure you can get home for a quick shave before your interview.

All candidates need to wear little to no cologne or perfume. Clothes that smell like cigarette smoke might offend the interviewer if they have a sensitive nose. Take out any facial jewelry and cover tattoos with long sleeves. Put your water bottle into a briefcase and leave the backpack in the car.

Lateness

The person who called and asked you for an interview will ask you if you need directions to the building. NEVER refuse these directions. Even if you think you know their location, you need to know *exactly* where you are going.

If you are not familiar with that particular area, it is still a great idea to drive there before you have to go for the interview. Map out directions and see how long it is going to take you to get there. Even if you have a GPS, getting specific from a person who goes there all the time will give you more backup than the GPS.

Remember to add a few minutes for traffic or other unforeseen delays. Try to arrive at least ten to fifteen minutes early. When you schedule your interview, make sure you know who will be interviewing you. The person who calls to set up the interview isn't always the person who does the interviews. Ask their name, title, and phone number. Put this information into your cell phone to have available in case a problem comes up. This way, you can contact them directly.

- Arrival time

Just like other issues during the interview process, determining the right time to arrive is tricky. One rule you need to remember is being late, even "casually late", will never be acceptable. Lateness is one of the main reasons interviewers don't hire someone for the job. If there aren't any extenuating circumstances, you always need to arrive early. If there are circumstances, call the interviewer and tell them that you are going to be a bit late.

The best time to get to your interview is about ten to fifteen minutes early. Anything less and you will be cutting it close. If you get there too soon, you will look too anxious. Remember: you are also taking up other people's time. If might even be that if you arrive on time, the interviewer might not be ready to talk with you. When you do arrive, if you are told that it will be a few minutes, take this time to use the restroom, compose yourself, and wait patiently.

- Call ahead

Give the person doing the interview a call as soon as you realize you are going to be late. The sooner you get in front of the damage control, the better off you will be.

If you have inadvertently left the interviewer's number at home, call the company and let somebody there know. They should be able to pass your message on to the correct person. Just simply say, "Hi, my name is… I have an interview for the position of… at two p.m. I am running a bit late. I'll be there as soon as I can."

There might be some situations when calling ahead isn't possible—like you had a car accident. You are going to be preoccupied, and this is understandable. With that being said, do try to call the company and tell them at your earliest convenience.

- Apologize

If you have ever waited two hours for a friend to make their appearance to your dinner party, which you spent an entire week getting ready for, it will be safe to say that your frustration level will be over the top. Even more so if they don't apologize.

Now think about doing that to an employer who has taken 30 minutes out of their day to talk to you about your experience to see if you will be a good fit for the company. Even if you're only ten minutes late, you can, at the very least, acknowledge this and give them a sincere apology for messing up their day.

- Prove that you are adaptable

Think about this scene from the movie *The Pursuit of Happiness*:

Christopher Gardner drags himself into an interview; it is going to end up changing his life while he wears a tank top splattered with paint after he has spent the night in jail. Even though he isn't appropriately dressed, he professionally conducts himself and can impress his future bosses. Not only does he prove that he is better than his tattered outfit, but he also demonstrates that he is adaptable.

50% of any job interview is about the interviewer getting to know who you are as a person, and getting a good feel for how you are going to fit within the company. How you can handle yourself under the pressure of being late to your interview is going to say a lot about who you are and how you will conduct yourself if you get the job. If you end up being late to your job interview, there is a good chance that you might end up being late to a meeting with a client, and the company is interested to see how well you can recover. When you walk in late, it turns into a test of how well you can handle this unfortunate situation.

If you do find yourself in the uncomfortable position of showing up late to your interview, all might not be lost. Make sure you are prepared and work through the situation like a professional; you might end up saving the interview and your job opportunity.

- A good reason for being late

Most of the time, the interviewer isn't going to ask why you are late, but you need to give them a reason anyway. It needs to be a good one. "Sorry, I didn't hear the alarm" or "I'm stuck in traffic" isn't going to cut it. Neither is: "I'm having a bad day"; "My cat coughed up a hairball on my blouse"; "My washing machine flooded the floor"; "I left only to realize that I was wearing two different shoes"; and "I ran back inside to change my shoes and then my car wouldn't start."

Interviewers are not the unforgiving monsters that we think they are. They know that life happens. If the reason you are late to your interview is something that couldn't be avoided, like a family emergency or a flat tire, then don't make up silly excuses.

The thing to remember is to give them information. Honesty has always been the best way to go.

- Give them an arrival time

Sending an email or calling ahead is not going to do much if you don't tell them how soon you will be there. Just saying, "I'll be there as soon as possible" is nothing. This could mean ten minutes away, or the train hasn't left the station.

They aren't asking for an exact time, but you need to give them a good estimate. Making them sit there wondering where you are or when you will get there might be a deal breaker. You don't want that to happen.

When you give them your arrival time, try to figure out the amount of time you need actually to get there. Then add on about five minutes for a buffer. Never tell them you have added in buffer time.

- Get ready to reschedule

The interviewer has set this time aside to talk with you, and you probably aren't the only person they are talking to that day. Their time is just as valuable as yours.

When you call to let them know you are going to be late, you need to be prepared for them to reschedule or cancel the interview. They have other things to do than to cater to your needs.

What is worse is that they go ahead and talk with the other candidate who showed up extremely early for their interview. They did show up very early, but at least they showed up before the interview's scheduled time.

- Take a moment to get yourself composed

Once you finally make it to the interview, it is imperative that you take a few moments to compose yourself before heading to the reception desk.

You might already be late, but taking a few minutes to check your appearance can make all the difference. You don't want to walk in with your hair mussed, your shirt untucked, and generally looking disheveled. Take a few deep breaths to calm your nerves to gain some brownie points. You don't have anything to lose.

Say, "I am confident and strong. I am a woman/man who thrives on new challenges and works hard to achieve my goals."

Now, go get 'em, tiger!

- Apologize again

When you finally meet the interviewer and extend your hand for a handshake, tell them you are sorry once more for keeping them waiting. Go easy on the apologies; you don't want to appear too desperate.

Know that this second chance is almost impossible, don't waste time by continually drawing attention to being late. Don't lose focus on why you are there: to show them how awesome you are and to get the job of your dreams.

- Send them a thank you note

You should already be planning to send them a thank you note after the interview. It doesn't matter what time you showed up. You need to take this time to apologize for your lateness again, along with your gratitude for taking the time to have the interview even after you showed up late.

Try to stick to just a few lines.

Try this:

"Dear, Hiring Manager,

Thank you so much for taking the time to meet with me today. I just wanted to apologize one more time for being late. It is not the way I ordinarily conduct myself.

I know this was inconvenient for you and I appreciate how you still took time out of your day to meet with me.

Once again, it was a pleasure, and I'm excited about everything I learned about the company and the role today.

Best regards,

(First and last name)

The best advice is not to be late—if at all possible. Get your clothes ready the night before, and anything else you might need, and leave your house 30 minutes earlier than you usually would. Do whatever it takes to make sure you get there ten minutes early.

Cell Phone Etiquette

In this day and age, our cell phones have become an extension of our body. We hardly ever find ourselves without them. In a study performed by Pew Research Center in 2015, they found that 46% of Americans "couldn't live without" their cell phones. Zogby's survey found that 87% of millennials claim that they are never separated from their phones.

Our cell phones hold cameras, parts of our social lives, entertainment, and calendars. However, when you are getting ready to head into a job interview, do the right thing and turn them off.

When it comes to making sure you have good cell phone etiquette during a job interview, there is one basic tip:

Turn off your phone.

This is extremely simple, yet most people forget or fail to do it. If needed, set a reminder on your phone to turn it off right before your interview. You should also make sure that your phone is completely off—don't put it on vibrate. If your phone were to go off, that buzzing noise is not only going to be distracting, but it will also be embarrassing mid-interview. All of those emails, calls, and texts can wait.

You have done all the hard work to get the interview. You have spent time getting things together for the interview. And you have the perfect laid out plan. However, if you go into that interview and the moment you open your mouth to introduce yourself, your phone starts ringing and playing, "If you like Pina Coladas" at a deafening level, it's probably going to be very hard to recover. This is one example of something that you don't want to end up happening during your job interview. This can be avoided by *turning off your phone.*

You should also make sure you turn off your phone early. Ideally, you need to shut your phone off while you are in your car and then leave the phone there. If you take public transport, turn off your phone before you walk into the building. This is a critical time for first impressions. You will probably be greeted by a receptionist when you walk in, so make sure that you focus on putting your best foot forward. Resist the urge of grabbing your phone if you have to wait a few minutes before you get called back into your interview. Many business reception areas have information about the company in their pictures or other written materials. You should have already done your research about the company, but take some time to read the things in the waiting area.

Take some time practicing being without your phone. Most of the behaviors we have when it comes to our cell phones have become subconscious. We automatically reach into our pockets to make sure that our phone is where it is supposed to be, or when somebody else gets a text. If you keep your phone in your briefcase or car, it will prevent you from doing these things. Take a couple of hours and leave your cell phone someplace that you can't easily access it and see how it feels. Go out with some family or friends and shut your phone off and leave it in your bag—just like you will do during the interview. As a bonus, you might remember what it is like to have an uninterrupted conversation.

That notebook and pen that you should have with you will also serve as a place to write down reminders. When the interviewer gives you information about things, you are going to need to write it in your notebook instead of reaching for your phone to type it out. After the interview, you can transfer the information to your cell phone.

Don't start checking your phone. This means you shouldn't sneak out into the hallway or bathroom to check what is going on in "Facebook land". You are currently in a building that is filled with people who could end up being your coworkers. You want to make a great first impression with everybody there. If you are planning on using your cell phone to send out that thank you note after your interview, wait until you get home or are in your car. It is a good idea to take some time to reflect on your interview before the thank you.

Living without your cell phone is hard. We have all become super dependent on technology. It helps us live our lives, and even your prospective employer understands. However, the odds of them going from prospective boss to current boss is greater if your phone doesn't end up going off in the middle of the interview while they are still getting to know you.

What happens if you do forget to turn off your phone, or at the very least, only silence it so that it doesn't make a noise just vibrates? If you ended up not taking any precautions and your phone does start buzzing or ringing while in the interview, the best thing to do is to turn it off quickly and apologize. Don't take the time to check who it was and don't try to create some lame excuse. The best thing to do is silence it, turn it off, and apologize.

Now, for every rule, there is always an exception or two. If the interviewer specifically asks you to use your phone so that they can view your profiles or social media, then this is okay. This could happen if there is a common friend or if social media plays a part in the job's role that you are applying for.

Finally, the only other reason to still have your phone on is if you are waiting for a severe medical or family call. If this is the case, make sure you tell the interviewer beforehand. They will be more accommodating if you are upfront with this information as if you are interrupted by a phone call, it is going to be expected, and they won't judge you for it.

Tests

You should be pretty well prepared for your interview by this point, but there is one thing that we need to talk about before moving onto the interview itself.

You have likely heard some stories, which have reached urban legend status, about how interviewers can be sadistic and force their interviewees to water for two hours before seeing them. While there may be some truth in the years of job interviews that a candidate was forced to wait for a while, you can almost be sure that it wasn't done intentionally.

That being said, having an interviewee wait five to ten more minutes is something that some interviewers will do. This doesn't mean that they do this to watch you squirm for a little while; this is just a way for an interviewer to know how you might react when things don't go as you expected.

They watch to see if you sit their patiently and stay relaxed and calm. Or, do you go up to the receptionist and start asking or demanding for the interviewer to see you immediately. Or do you decide to storm out after having to wait just a few extra minutes? How you react to this situation before you are hired can end up determining how you are going to react to similar problems once you have been hired.

Since you will probably have a bit of wait-time—if you do show up at the suggested five to ten minutes earlier than your scheduled time—bring along a book or magazine to keep you entertained. Make sure that it is something that you wouldn't be embarrassed to be caught reading. Above everything else, make sure that you don't show annoyance. If the receptionist tells you that it is going to be a couple more minutes, simply respond graciously as if nothing has happened, and then keep your focus on your book or magazine.

These few minutes are probably going to be some of the hardest minutes in your life. Up to this point, you have spent your time getting your things together, dressing, eating, and getting to your interview. Now everything has come to a halt. This halt often causes the best of us to fidget. Resist this temptation. Fidgeting is the last thing that you want to be caught doing. You want to come off as confident and show the company and interviewer that you are the type of person who can handle changes and challenges, not the least of which is having to wait for somebody.

Common Mistakes During the Interview

During the hiring process, you have to know what you shouldn't do during a job interview. This is as important as having strong references and a polished resume.

Just like any other interpersonal interactions, job interviews could be very subjective. Experts have found some common interview mistakes that you have to avoid to improve the chances of having a great interview and making a good impression.

Not Knowing About the Company

You need to approach your job interview just like you would a test. It is essential to study the company you are applying to work for so you can talk about your skills and knowledge regarding being a good fit for the business.

To stand out from the crowd, do enough research so you can talk about their recent merger. It shows you are passionate about the company and the role.

Not having the basic knowledge of the role you are applying for or giving them good examples about their past performance makes you look like you have shown up after finding the company on a Google search.

Interviewers like to ask fundamental questions about your interest in the company, your skills, and your background, along with why you think you would be a good fit.

At the bare minimum, read up on the company and have some anecdotes prepared about some projects you have completed successfully.

You also need to know your interviewer. Be prepared with information about the person who will be conducting the interview. You might find that you have a shared interest you will be able to talk about and build rapport from. You might even realize the interviewer has connections to some of your previous employers.

Besides being thoroughly prepared, it might help to calm your nerves. You gain confidence from being competent.

Not Being Yourself

Now is not the time to be humble. Never assume the interviewer is going to remember each detail from your resume about all the sales goals you reached or the awards you won. Women are known to deflect credit about their accomplishments and need to practice talking about their talents and qualifications.

Not Making Eye Contact

Communication is key in an interview. It is crucial to make eye contact when being spoken to and when speaking. Offer them a firm handshake and sit with a correct posture. Even though you might be nervous, try not to let your nervous energy cause you to fidget.

Common Questions and Wrong Answers

People being interviewed should not bring up the salary first—since it puts them in a weak position to negotiate. Bringing it up too soon might give the interviewer the impression that you are only interested in the perks of the job. Save this for after the job has been offered to you.

You need to be prepared to talk about what salary you do expect just in case they bring up the topic.

- Biggest weakness

When your interviewer asks about your biggest weakness, do not offer them a cute answer like, "I work too hard." Instead, this implies that you are not entirely self-aware or aren't taking them seriously, or can't deal with constructive criticism.

Have an honest but thoughtful answer along with an explanation about how you are working to improve your biggest weakness.

Not Asking Questions or Showing Interest

Many interviewers will leave time toward the end to answer questions for you. Usually, they know that you are examining them as well and want to make it a two-sided conversation. This is also a small test. What questions you ask will reveal how you think and the things that are important to you. It will show that you care enough and would like to know more.

It is a good idea to ask questions throughout the interview to keep it an organic, flowing conversation.

Declining to ask questions can be a fatal mistake; it tells them that you aren't interested in the company, or you think you know everything about them already.

Not preparing any questions also shows them that you don't care, haven't done any homework, or aren't curious. If you freeze up and can't think of one, use an old standby like, "What's the culture like here?" or "What does success look like in this role?"

When they wrap up the interview and ask you if you have any questions, you can reply with something like, "I have many questions, and I'm afraid I might run out of time, so I'll just jump right in."

It will show them you have a great interest in the company.

- Not asking about what comes next

At the end of the interview, if they don't give you any information about what comes next in the process, ask. This shows that you are very interested and will keep you informed.

Talking Badly About Previous Employers

Nothing shows you have a bad attitude like criticizing your past or current employer. The person doing the interview is going to wonder if you will talk about them or the company if they do or don't hire you.

Coming Off Desperate, Arrogant, or Unenthusiastic

You never want to come on too strong, brag until you begin sounding arrogant, and dominate the conversation. Some people who are in marketing or sales usually have strong personalities and take over the interview. You want to examine the interviewer, but you can't let them know you are doing it, as you will be seen as an overbearing control freak.

- Talking over others

Don't you love being in a group of people, and one of them talks over everyone else and takes over the conversation? Think about a person who fits this description. Now, would you want to interview this type of person? The odds are you won't.

If you are an excessive talker, you have to know when to share the conversation and when to close your mouth. If you do not, you will ruin your interview without even realizing it. The problem is that most people don't know they fit into this category.

- Talking too much

When you begin rambling, you waste the interviewer's time, and you won't be able to cover everything you want to. Communication skills are excellent to have for many positions, so the interviewer might be trying to see if you can talk with brevity and clarity.

Take the time to listen to the question that they are asking, and give them time to finish their sentence without interrupting them. Never end their sentences for them. When you do talk, notice the balance that you create when talking with them. If you don't, your interview might come to an abrupt close.

- Answers are too long

You might also ruin your interview if you give long answers to simple questions. This is common with any job seeker who has over twenty years of experience. You have much experience, but don't lose your interviewer's interest by telling them every single thing you have ever done.

Many interviewers want to hire candidates who work well in a team. They want a person who interacts well with coworkers and clients. People who talk too much don't fit into this description—since many people look at them as busybodies, forceful, and untrustworthy.

A leading cause of low employee morale and employee turnover goes back to poor management. Leaders have to set examples and show respect for their employees by making an environment where they feel their opinion is valued. Other staff members won't receive well constant talkers—since they tend to have a one-sided view of the way things need to run and have a hard time validating the opinions of others. This can cause workplace friction.

Sales managers are reluctant to hire constant talkers since they don't get favored by most of their clients. Why? They often force their opinions on them, have a hard time listening to others viewpoints, and are too focused on their agendas. They could cause the company to lose clients. If you are applying for a sales position, you have to listen to this advice. You have to demonstrate that you have effective communication skills all through the interview.

- Moments of silence

Don't get restless during silent moments, especially if there is a panel of interviewers. The interviewer/s might be thinking about their next question, taking notes, or thinking about your last reply. During these times, you don't need to continue to talk or start rambling about something irrelevant.

If your natural tendency is to talk a lot or fast, try to speak slower and pause to give others time to talk. You have to practice this a lot even when out with friends or family. Remember: being able to have a good conversation is knowing how to listen and when to talk.

- Showing low energy

This is an interview killer. Here is what it looks like: a lack of enthusiasm, slow to respond to questions, no or little eye contact, and slumped shoulders. If you want the job, showing these signs will make it impossible to persuade anyone to hire you.

- Too Arrogant

It doesn't matter how much experience you have, how attractive you are, or your education level; if you begin acting like you are more important or better than anyone else, most of the time, a company will not hire you.

It is hard to realize you might be arrogant if you cannot humble yourself and take an honest, hard look at your life, workplace environment, personal life, or friendships. If you are thought of as being arrogant or prideful, then the person doing the interview will see you this way too. There isn't anything wrong with being assertive and confident, but being overbearing and egotistical will bring the interview to a close quickly.

Don't confuse confidence and arrogance. A confident leader can discuss their accomplishments and experiences positively without having to belittle other people. They know they can achieve great things. They don't have to force any attention on to themselves since they can inspire others just by being themselves. Surprisingly, by the end of the interview, you might have inspired the interviewer too.

Arrogant leaders will irritate an interviewer. It will be hard for them to talk about their actions. They think their charm and wit will master the interview, but they are very wrong. Trying to be subtle doesn't work for an arrogant person. Interviewers can easily see this character flaw. If a weak area is pointed out, like little to no experience, that has a hard time responding without becoming condescending or exaggerating about accomplishments. Here is a sample:

Interviewer: "I see you have less than two years of experience in leading a global team. We are looking for people who have ten or more years of experience."

Applicant: "I don't think you need to have many years of experience leading a global team to know what you are doing. I have been doing this for less than two years, and my team is now leading in sales as a result of some new systems I implemented. Now all the managers who have been doing this for many years come to me for advice."

You might think there isn't anything wrong with the applicant's answer but look closer. His answer might be correct, but the delivery is entirely wrong. To paraphrase, he has told the interviewer that "you don't need much experience," and that they "don't know what they are talking about since I am number one, everyone asks my advice, and I am the new kid on the block." Here is a better way to answer the question:

Interviewer: "I see that you have less than two years of experience in leading a global team. We are looking for people who have ten or more years of experience."

Applicant: "Yes, that is true, and I have learned a lot during this time. I am very pleased to see that my division is now leading the region in sales in a short time. I highly respect the other seasoned managers who have been doing this for a long time, and I am humbled that they now ask my advice to learn about some systems my team and I have implemented."

Did you see the difference? This second one says the same thing but has a balance of humility and confidence that will make the interviewer like the person more. They are saying the same thing without being arrogant. They also gave respect to other workers who have more years of experience. Instead of them taking complete ownership of the success and new system, they also gave credit to their team.

Here are some responses to stay away from:

1. Brag response

It is fine to sell yourself and convince the interviewer that you are the best person for the job, but you have to avoid exaggerating your accomplishment. Never make an interviewer feel bad when they ask an obvious question.

They might ask if you have any marketing experience, and you respond with laughter and say, "That's all I have done for the past ten years." Understand that all interviewers are professionals; if you make them feel inadequate, the interview is finished.

2. "I" response

If you always start a sentence with "I" instead of "we" or "our", you are doing more harm than good. When you overuse the word "I", it might be interpreted as you "loving to take credit for everything". Start watching out for this if you are interviewing for a job that is part of a team.

3. Professor response

If anyone has ever told you that you respond like you are condescending or lecturing, you have to work on your presentation skills. This happens when people who have big egos give complicated long answers rather than brief replies.

These people get pleasure when they explain complex, intricate details about their jobs. If this sounds like you, try working on your tone, simplify your answers, and ease up on the attitude. Interviewers don't like to feel as if they are listening to a lecture.

- Getting to the interview late

Because candidates for a job usually have interviews with different managers that are scheduled one after the other, two things might happen if you show up late: your first interview might be cut short, or you disrupt other interviewer's schedule. Neither one will be good for you because it will either make many people upset or shorten your interview time.

- Forgetting to follow up

Many people forget the basic rule of interviewing: Follow up within one day by email to thank them for the interview, their time, and to show you are very interested in the role. If you don't, the hiring manager might think you aren't organized or interested. They might just forget about you.

- Arriving too early

Looking at the other side of it, getting to the interview too early can also make the hiring manager mad because it disrupts their schedule. It is a good idea to get there ten minutes early to get through security (if they have it) and check in with the receptionist. It allows you time to use the restroom, prepare for the interview, and compose yourself. It is a gross mistake to get there any earlier than fifteen minutes before your interview.

- Asking personal questions

Some people get so nervous that they forget etiquette and get too personal with their questions. Never ask an interviewer why they left their previous job for their current one, where they have worked, or any details about their family. These questions might make the interviewer feel very uncomfortable and does not show them anything about you.

- Following up aggressively

Yes, it is vital that you follow up, but you shouldn't send multiple emails or call the interviewer. It is very awkward to get a call from somebody who demands to know why they haven't heard back from you. Send them an email and move on with your life. Anything more than one email is way too much.

- Focusing on themselves

If you look at things from the perspective of the employer, the job interview is supposed to help them determine whether or not you will be a good match for the needs of the company. This means your answers need to focus on how the company is going to benefit from your expertise and how you are going to benefit from having the job.

Talking on and on about what you want, how this job is the right direction for your career, and how this experience will be great for you is entirely meaningless to the person doing the interview.

Companies don't hire you to help you; they hire you because you have skills that will help them reach their goals. Your responses will show how you can help the company.

Use a friendly tone but make sure you don't cross the line by sharing too much information. Remember: you don't know how the interviewer will react to being told about your weekend shenanigans. You only get so much time, so you need to remain focused on your accomplishments and the needs of the company.

- Using your cell phone

Even if you are only seeing what time it is, looking at your cell phone might show them you are easily distracted, or rude. Before going into the interview, turn off any devices and put them away. You might be used to taking notes with your phone, but during a job interview, use a notebook.

- Gushing

Never overcompliment the company or the interviewer. You might begin to sound disingenuous.

- Getting angry or desperate

Having these traits is very unattractive to interviewers. It doesn't matter how strongly you might hate your current job or how desperate you are to get a new job; you have to keep your emotions under control during an interview.

Lying to Get the Job

Do you like being lied to? Of course not. And the person interviewing you isn't going to like it either. Saying you are qualified for something when you are not will cause big problems in your future. This never turns out right. When the company finds out the truth, and they will, you will get fired.

Experienced human resource managers are very familiar with deceitful practices like inaccurate accomplishments, incorrect salary, imprecise education, misleading skill sets, wrong job titles, exaggerated employment dates, and false company listings.

So many people throw away wonderful job opportunities because they decided to lie on their resume, during the interview, or on the job application. Many will get away with it, and most HR departments can't investigate every single applicant, but if you continuously do this and don't change, the chances are that one day you will have to confront the truth. It is possible for you not to get the job or lose it after you were hired if you lied during the application process.

Think about how it would feel to get a phone call from your interviewer after they have gotten your background check and they tell you that your employment dates are wrong, and they can't offer you the job because of that.

Another example of lying is rounding off or increasing your hourly wage. If you make $17.30 an hour, don't be tempted to record it as $18 an hour. This goes for employees who are on a salary too. If you earn $53,000 per year and get a bonus of $10,000, don't record your annual base salary as $63,000.

Your best approach is always honesty. Use job skills and experience as your bargaining tools instead of an exaggerated pay scale to adjust income. Also, use your commissions and bonus structure as a way of negotiating a job offer.

Just remember that deceitfulness and lying won't just damage your credibility but can cause you to lose the job. In many cases, like in executive positions, references can't be done until the employee has given their notice to leave their current job. Could you imagine giving your current employer your notice and then realizing that your prospective employer has taken away the job offer? This happens more often than most people realize.

Here is an example of what lying about your skills could do to your future:

A man goes to a job interview and tells his potential employer that he is an expert at programming. To be truthful, his skill set is only in the beginner to intermediate level. He is hired and given the position of programming manager. They offer him a six-figure annual salary. He quits his current job, buys a house, marries his long-time girlfriend, and thinks life is fantastic.

Within one month, he is fired from his position because his employer finds out that he doesn't know much about the specific programming skill he said he was an expert at.

The man thought he could deceive his employer by saying the right words to get through the interview. However, once he had to do the task in front of his boss, he finally admitted that he didn't know how to run the program. Thus, he lost his job.

You have to remember to be honest about what information you give to prospective employers to steer clear of unfortunate and embarrassing circumstances.

Never lie; it is that simple. If you didn't finish that degree because you are missing one class, don't say you have the education requirements. If you don't have a specific skill, don't lie and risk getting exposed. Remain truthful and bring confidence to the interview. Know that you were hired because you represented yourself truthfully and they are getting everything you said you are.

Looking Unpolished

Many people will form an opinion of you in the first seven seconds of meeting you. That doesn't mean you have to wear a designer suit or dress for a job interview for an executive or management position; however, you do need to know some things about the corporate climate and culture of the company before you reach into your closet and grab that perfectly tailored suit or dress.

For some, this won't be a big problem—since you know how to dress for interviews within your industry. But know that all employers and industries aren't the same. What might be acceptable in one environment might be a huge mistake in another.

Dressing too fancy might make you stand out and ruin any chance of getting hired. What do you think would happen if you walked into a machine shop in a tailored suit for an interview. It won't go down too well because most of the people in the place are going to look at you like you are afraid of "getting your hands dirty".

It is imperative to know the culture and climate of a company before you decide how to dress. It is unfortunate that people are so judgmental, but they are. You don't want to get picked on just because of the way you dressed.

Here is an example of dressing too nice:

Early on in a recruiter's career, the recruiter advises a woman, who is about to interview for a management position, to wear a nice dress. The recruiter thinks the woman looks very nice and appropriately attired. Later on that day, the interviewer calls the recruiter and tells them they aren't sure the woman is the right fit for the company. They say their company is very laid back and she was overdressed. Nobody could get past how nice she had dressed. The interviewer also tells the recruiter how their customers are also laid back and prefer a manager who doesn't look like a shiny sales representative.

The recruiter is baffled; they have tons of experience and were confident that the woman was perfect for the job. They can't believe the company is throwing away a perfect candidate just because of the way she was dressed. It makes no sense at all. The recruiter tries every way possible to change the company's mind. They remind them of all the experience the woman has, but nothing will persuade them otherwise. They can't look past the tailored dress, patent leather shoes, designer briefcase, etc. The woman had put her best foot forward but, unfortunately, got rejected because the company could not relate to her. They formed an opinion of her in just seconds, and no amount of experience will change their minds.

Was this example fair? No! However, this is the world we live in. When you are interviewing for jobs, remember that people will hire someone they like and can relate to.

Now, on the other end of the scale, that doesn't mean you should wear jeans and a T-shirt to an interview for a managerial position. However, perhaps tone down your attire to a dress shirt, slacks, and maybe a jacket. That said, let's now talk about dressing too provocatively for an interview.

This is becoming a huge problem that nobody addresses. Interviewers are not going to tell you that your skirt is too short, your blouse is cut too low, or your clothing fits too tightly—not to your face anyway.

Once you leave the interview, you think you blew their minds, but what you don't realize is that the interview was over the moment you stepped into the room. Don't do this to yourself. Dress modestly and let the person conducting the interview focus on you, your resume, and your experience so they can see how great you are.

One more thing: go easy on colognes and perfumes. Yes, they might smell wonderful on you, but strong scents can be distracting. Plus, some people might be allergic to certain smells.

Everyone knows not to judge a book by its cover, but interviewers will. If you show up to an interview looking disheveled or too informal, you will make a bad impression before you even get the chance to introduce yourself.

When you look professional, it shows that you care about the interview and are trying to put your best foot forward. Too many people go to an interview with clothes that are stained, wrinkled, rumpled, and generally, do not fit. You don't have to look like you stepped out of the pages of a magazine, but you need to select your outfit carefully, fix your hair, and take a general look in the mirror before going to your interview.

Forgetting Your Resume

In a perfect world, the interviewer will have your resume ready in hand, but everyone's days are busy, and not everybody can be super organized. This means you always need to have a copy for every person you think you will meet, plus extras in case you get another interview. It is not just helpful but shows you are prepared and thoughtful.

Not Being Available During Business Hours

It might be hard to fit a job interview into your schedule if you are still working a full-time job. However, the interviewer wants to do the interviews during their working hours, so you need to be prepared to take a vacation day if necessary.

Being Rude

You need to try to make a good impression on anyone you meet. You don't know whose opinion will count during the hiring process.

You need to be nice to everybody because many people in management roles will ask the parking attendant, receptionist, and clients if you were respectful to them.

Talking About Illegal Activities

This is not the time to talk about your hobbies or recreational drug use that might violate the employer's conduct policies or laws.

Talking About the Interview On Social Media

Never post anything that you do not want your potential new employer to see. You might also end up tipping your current employer off with regards to how you are looking for a new job.

Bad Interviews

Once you have been asked to come in for an interview, it feels great. And it is. It is the first step to acquiring your dream job. However, to interviewers, it is just another day for them. Interviewers usually conduct hundreds, possibly thousands, of interviews every year. Being unprepared for the interview can be the "kiss of death" for many.

This isn't meant to discourage you or suggest that the people conducting the interview don't care. The main point is that they go through this process a lot more than you do. When you give them what you think is an exciting, unique, or thought-out response, they might have heard it many times in just one week. If you want to stand out, you have to avoid clichéd answers and dig deep into the information they are looking for.

There are many ways you can blow an interview. The worst answers can show the interviewer flaws with your preparation, attitude, and interest in the job qualifications to get the job done. They could also show you can't work well with others or you have a bad work ethic.

What responses are the worst offenders? Some of the answers are scary, and some are funny. It would be much better to get prepared and stay away from giving any of these answers during your job interview. We talked with many career coaches, HR professionals, recruiters, and other experts to get their opinion.

These answers to typical job interview questions show either a total lack of being prepared or no understanding of how to have a successful interview. Regardless, the results will always be the same: a lost opportunity. These are some answers to stay away from no matter what:

Q: Tell me about yourself?

A: Details about your professional flaws, medical history, or details about your family life.

"There isn't much to tell."

"I'm a rock musician. I'm a drummer. Our agent quit, and we don't have any gigs for the rest of the year. We are looking for a new agent, and I hope to get back to that soon. That is what I do."

"I am a huge Yankees fan, avid softball player, and I have the gift of gab. I'm usually the life of every party."

Q: What are your greatest strengths?

A: "I'm a team player."

"I don't know, but I am a good learner."

"I do good work."

"I'm the best."

Q: What do you know about the company?

A: Avoiding giving them a straight answer.

"I heard you pay well."

"You have a job opening."

Visible details like their industry.

Q: Why should we hire you?

A: "It sounded like a fun job."

"I am the best person for the job."

"I am a hard worker."

"I am great with people."

"I need a job."

"I need money."

"Nobody else will hire me."

"I'm desperate."

"I'm unemployed."

"I don't know."

Q: What are your most significant weaknesses?

A: "I'm not good with the newest version of Microsoft Office."

"I can't do spreadsheets."

"I don't like dealing with difficult people."

"I don't have any."

"I have a lot; it is hard to choose just one."

"I don't spell well."

"I'm a perfectionist."

"I work too hard."

"I can't think of any."

"I have been known to lose my patience with incompetent people."

Q: Tell me about your last job?

A: "You have my resume right there; didn't you read it?"

Q: Why do you want to work here?

A: "I need a job."

"My mom said I had to get a job."

"I hear you give great employee discounts."

"I look great in a uniform."

"I can walk to work from where I live."

Q: Why are you the right candidate for this position?

A: "I'm passionate about it."

Q: Where do you see yourself in five years?

A: "Still doing this job."

"Doing your job."

"I hate this question."

Q: What is your greatest strength?

A: "I'm a team player."

Q: Do you have any questions for me?

A: "How much is the employee discount?"

"How much vacation time do I get?"

"I don't have any questions."

"Do I have to work overtime?"

"No."

"Would you like to go out for a drink?"

"Is there a limit on how much I can buy?"

"Can I resell?"

"Do I get paid sick days? How many do I get every month?"

"How often do we get raises?"

"Do you conduct background checks?"

"Do you check references?"

"Do I have to pass a drug test before I get hired? How much notice do you give before the test?"

Q: Do you work well with others?

A: "I work fine with most people, but others bother me a lot."

"My coworkers don't like me, but I think it's because I intimidate them."

Q: Why did you apply for this position?

A: "I saw it in the jobs listings, and it seemed interesting."

Q: Why did you get fired?

A: "I missed too many days."

"I failed a drug test."

Q: What did you like least about your previous position?

A: "I hated the job and the company. They were awful to work for."

Good Interviews

You might be wondering what steps you can take to have a great job interview. Well, you have chosen the right book. This chapter will guide you through the whole process from getting yourself prepared, the day of the interview, what questions might be asked, and the waiting game after the interview.

Here is a secret that might help you relax a bit: the people conducting the interview actually want you to do well. It is not easy for them to find the perfect person for the job. You will make their day better if you wind up being the person they are looking for.

So, to prepare yourself, instead of looking at the interviewer as somebody who is trying to "mess you up", it will help if you thought about them as a person who is cheering you on. That doesn't mean some of them won't try and trip you up, but with the tips below, you will be ready for them.

Getting Ready for the Interview

What should you do to have a great job interview? Here are some tips that will help.

Remember that success begins before you even walk in the door.

1. Review the job description carefully

Look up everything that you don't understand. This helps you to make sure you answer all of their needs.

2. Make notes

Write down some notes using the job description and resume. Think about some stories that are related to the job you are applying for or from somewhere else if you think it will help you get your point across.

You can use these to show the interviewer how you have gone above and beyond to solve an issue, made a new method, overcome weaknesses, helped during a critical situation, or helped to reach a successful outcome. You might not have to use every story you know, but it is smart to have some just in case you need them.

3. Research the company

If you didn't look the company up before you applied for the job, you need to do so now. There isn't anything less impressive than chatting with someone without knowing anything about the company. If at all possible, look for information about the person who will be interviewing you. Use this information sparingly, or it might seem like you are stalking them. Use GlassDoor.com or LinkedIn to help with research. They can give you some great insights.

4. Practice

Answer the most popular interview questions that you will find later in this chapter to help you. Do this in front of a mirror or have a friend do some mock interviews with you.

You need to be comfortable talking about yourself and all the things you have accomplished that you can bring to the company. Try not to sound like you are bragging or are too self-conscious. Be yourself and remember you are only having a conversation with another person.

5. Know your resume

You would be amazed at the number of people who have stuttered when asked about the experience they have listed on their resume. It is surprising to interview someone who can't remember what they have listed on their resume or when they learned a specific skill.

Interview Day

1. Turn off your cell phone

This is easy to forget, but it isn't necessarily a deal breaker. It might be for some, but it is annoying. Try to remember to turn it off or leave it in your car or purse.

2. Dress professionally

Match your look to what you know about the company and what they require. Look them up online or go by the company to see how their employees dress. If they allow casual dress like T-shirts and jeans, don't wear this to the interview though. Wear a pair of nice slacks or a skirt along with a dress shirt and jacket. A suit would be too formal.

Don't be too much: haute couture (even if this is the type of job, don't try to wow them), avant-garde, casual, elegant, or sexy (cover up the assets). Less is always more here.

3. Resume

Always bring extra copies of your resume. Professionals do misplace things.

4. Feeling nervous

If you begin to feel super nervous before you leave for your interview, try doing some exercise. You don't want to go all out and get super sweaty, especially if you know you won't have time to shower. Singing or some simple jumping jacks can help get rid of the jitters. Nerves are very normal and okay since nerves can be channeled into other energy.

Meditation or yoga can help too. Believing in yourself and being prepared is the best medicine.

5. While you are waiting

While you are sitting in the waiting area don't prop your feet up on chairs or tables, slurp your coffee, slump, put on makeup, hum, scroll through your tablet or phone, chew gum, or—seriously—have parents or children with you. It's amazing how often this happens.

You have to be prepared to wait patiently, no matter for how long. Look as energized and pleasant as possible. Use this time to think about your stories and how your experience will fit in with the company. Observe everything you can during this time because you are trying to decide if you want to work here too.

6. The receptionist is a great ally

At least they shouldn't try to sabotage you. You might be wondering how this is important, but it is reminding you of one important fact: what comes out of your mouth is just one part of the interview process; first impressions are a huge part of the interview.

The interview isn't going to begin when the person doing the interview walks into the room and shakes your hand. It also doesn't end when you walk out of their office. Anybody at any step of this process can share information about you. Be nice to everyone.

7. Remain positive

No matter the context, always remain levelheaded and positive throughout the interview process. Getting angry or annoyed by small or trivial things, such as the interviewer not smiling at you, won't do you any favors. Instead, it will kill your chances of getting the job.

What Not To Say

1. Look the interviewer in the eye

When the interviewer walks into the room, look them in the eye, smile, and shake their hand. When shaking hands, don't go for the death grip, just a nice firm shake. Say something nice.

2. Never lie

Don't ever lie, even if you have to admit you don't know something. If it is applicable, show interest in learning about new things. You could tell the interviewer that you have started looking into it and add your question about what they just asked. This shows you are truly interested. A good employer doesn't expect you to know everything.

3. Never use canned answers

When you are in an interview, trust that you have done everything possible up to that moment. Answer in YOUR words and make sure you heard correctly what they asked. People looking for a job will overprepare themselves to the point that they put a canned answer to a question that wasn't asked.

This is never a good idea. It tells the interviewer you aren't listening. Turn to your stories, but be conversational. Too many memorized words will lose the human connection you are trying to build.

4. Never say you don't have questions for them

Don't ever tell them that you don't have any questions for them. Prepare some questions in advance. Feel free to take some notes and use things you have learned during the interview to find a question. This earns big points.

For the final question, if you feel things have gone well, let them know how interested you are and ask when they might get back in touch with you.

5. Stay away from jokes

Jokes can fall flat at times. Humor is fine if it feels right and if the interviewer is funny. Feel free to laugh at their jokes. Never, ever, fake laugh. They will see right through it. Do a small chuckle or smile.

Winning an interview

1. Look them in the eye

When you walk into the interview, shake the interviewer's hand and smile. Never shake hands like you are trying to rip their hand off. Just something firm and friendly.

2. Use real-life stories

You have researched the company. You have read the job description. Make sure you can match your experience and stories to what the company is looking for. Tell them how you have solved problems.

3. Practice

Before the day of your interview, go through standard interview questions with someone you trust.

4. More than one interviewer

If there is more than one person in the room while you are being interviewed, direct the answer to the person who asked the question. Be sure to make eye contact with every person at some point.

5. Speak clearly

Speak at a normal conversational pace. Remember to breathe.

6. Keep eye contact

Maintain eye contact, keep the energy up, and listen. If you realize you are beginning to think ahead about how to answer, or what they might ask later, stop yourself. You are going to lose more than you gain by jumping ahead. Trust yourself and stay in the moment. Make a connection and show them that you will be an asset to their team.

7. Still nervous?

If you are still feeling a bit nervous, it is fine to mention you are nervous if you think it might help get rid of some of the discomfort. The interviewer expects nerves. Add in some words about how excited you are for the opportunity. Stay brief and move on and answer their questions.

8. When the interview is over

Remember to smile and shake hands once the interview is over. Shake hands with everyone in the room and thank each person.

After the Interview

1. Thank you note

Some people say this isn't important. It might not be in many cases, and it probably isn't going to change your chances. If you send one, though, make it short and pleasant. It will leave a great impression. Snail mail is excellent, but email is fine too.

2. Follow up

After the interview is over, the time you wait to hear if you've been successful will test the patience of the most confident and most energetic person. It might take a day, or even months to hear back from them, even if you were their top candidate. Even in the best of circumstances, it might go beyond what they told you it would, especially if more than one person is making the decisions.

This is when you need to continue to look and find things to keep yourself occupied. Once a couple of weeks have passed, and you still haven't heard from them, it is fine to call and inquire about your status. Let them know you are still interested. You could also ask if there is anything else you can give them to make their decision easier.

They usually never forget. Even if you didn't follow up or send them a thank you, if you are the best candidate, they will contact you.

How to Improve Your Interview Skills

The best way to improve your skills is to do practice interviews. Ask a friend to pretend they are interviewing you. Don't allow them to take it easy on you either. Run it like a real interview. Record yourself so you can watch it later.

Most Common Questions

How many questions your interviewer asks could be limitless. The following is a list of the most commonly asked questions and how you can answer them in ways that will make you more memorable. Even the standard questions can have smart answers.

Take the time to read through all of these questions and think about them carefully. Think about how you would answer them if asked. Being prepared is the key to success. Not being prepared is a grave mistake; it shows the potential employer that you don't have any interest. Prepare your answers to these common questions:

- Tell me about yourself

This isn't a question but an invitation to share things about yourself that you think are important. Talk about why you worked at specific jobs. Say why you left them. Explain why you went to a certain school and grad school. What were your reasons behind it? Explain why you backpacked through Europe for one year and what you learned from the experience. While answering the questions, connect the dots on your resume so the interviewer can understand not only what you have done but why you did it. This is your chance to show how you are different from the other candidates.

- What are your weaknesses?

Everyone knows the way to answer this: choose weakness and magically change it into a strength.

Here is an example of an answer: "My biggest weakness is being too absorbed in my work that I lose all track of time. Each day I look up and realize everybody else has gone home. I know I should be more aware of the clock, but when I love what I'm doing, I can't think about anything else."

This means that your biggest weakness is that you put in more hours than everybody else. That's great; however, a better way to approach this is to choose an actual weakness that you are trying to improve and tell the interviewer what you have been doing to overcome it. Nobody is perfect, but if you can show them that you are honestly willing to look at yourself and find ways to improve, you will get pretty close.

- Where do you see yourself in five years?

Your interviewer doesn't care that you want to be a supervisor and climb the corporate ladder. If you aren't interviewing for a supervisory position, they don't care about your management skills. You can tell them how you have mentored others and led projects without supervision. That shows them you have leadership skills.

You could tell them something like how in five years you could make a huge impact on the company's future. Think about ways you can do this in the position that you are interviewing for. If you are interviewing for a career in technology, you need to advance your skills here too. You also need to share the areas you need to strengthen. Make sure these areas of expertise are what the company is needing.

- What are your strengths?

Not sure why interviewers insist on asking this question since they are looking at your resume and it shows your strengths. However, if you are asked this question, give them an on point, sharp answer. Be precise and clear. If you are great at solving problems, don't tell them that; instead, give them some examples that can prove you are great at solving problems. If you are an intelligent, emotional leader, also don't tell them that; instead, give them some examples that show you know how to answer their unasked questions.

Don't claim to have specific attributes; you have to prove the attributes to them.

- Why should we hire you?

This is a differentiation question. They want you to tell them that they would be crazy not to hire you.

Let them know that you possess almost all the experience they are looking for and you have a few extra abilities that they don't know they need as of yet. Make them understand that you are a person who will not only meet their needs but will be a valuable asset for the future.

Will they need a different set of skills as the company grows?

You might have skills that you saw in a different job description they want to fill.

You can mention this, and they might let you help with some of those jobs until they find somebody to hire for that position or you could be the new hire's backup.

Have you done some things that they are just now beginning? Having these "skills" to offer is a great plus for any job candidate.

- How do others describe you?

Here is another opportunity to diversify yourself. Everybody says they are a team player, good communicator, and a hard worker.

How many are leaders in their industry, game changers, and problem solvers?

Get creative and have stories to tell. Your interviewer wants to know why somebody thinks you are any of the above.

You want to give them attributes that show them you are the go-to person no matter where you work. Even normal answers can be tweaked to make you more valuable:

> 1. Yes, they want people who will work hard, but that is normal for any workplace. You might work hard, but you help others work smarter, not harder. You help them do their jobs better, and this makes their jobs much easier.

> 2. Anybody can communicate well. This doesn't just mean speaking well; this also includes listening. Are you always hearing things that other people don't? Can you understand how to do things fast? Do you understand what people are trying to tell you with body language and other clues?

> 3. Every job expects you to be a team player. What does being a team player mean? Does it mean you have to get along with everybody? This isn't hard to do if you are nice. What about pulling your weight? This is again expected. What have you accomplished that goes beyond your job description that helped the team meet that impossible deadline, and what did you do that saved your team from disaster?

- How did you hear about the job opening?

Job fairs, online listings, general postings, job boards—most people find their job this way, so it isn't a wrong answer. A person who continually finds each job from general postings just hasn't figured out what they want to do. They are only looking for any job they can find.

Don't explain how you heard about the job; *show* them you heard about it because you either follow the company, heard about it from one of their current employees, or through a colleague. Show them you knew about the job because you wanted to work there.

Companies don't want to hire someone who only wants a job; they want to hire somebody who wants to work at their company.

- When can you start?

You have to be careful about how you answer this question for many reasons:

This doesn't mean you have the job. They might want to know to put it in their notes. You have to keep your guard up until you have finished the interview and are driving away.

If you are still employed at another company, you need to be honest about the start date and show some professionalism. You need to tell them you have to talk with your current company and see if they require specific notice before leaving the job. If you have a crucial role in the company, your new employer will expect a transition period too.

If you can begin right away, by all means, tell them tomorrow. Having a sense of urgency and excitement about beginning work for a new company is a great thing.

- Why do you want this particular job?

This answer should be a heartfelt one, and your gut will give you the answer. If your answer has to do with benefits, work schedule, location, money, or other factors that don't have anything to do with the job, you might want to think a bit more. These reasons are not relevant to the interviewer.

You need to dig deep on this answer. Don't just talk about why the company will be a great one to work for. Talk to them about how the position will be a perfect fit for what you want to accomplish both long and short term.

They want to hear that this is your dream job. This job is your next step toward your desired career.

Be ready for their follow up question: How so?

You need to answer this honestly and tell them exactly how this job meets your professional needs and how you can contribute to your highest ability while at the company. People like to feel as if their work means something. There isn't anything wrong with sharing your feelings thoughtfully.

If you can't figure out why the position will be a perfect fit, you need to look elsewhere. Life is too short.

- Tell me about your dream job?

There are three words that you need to use to answer this question: relevance, relevance, relevance.

This doesn't mean you have to make up an answer. You should be able to learn something from each job you have. Try to work backward; find things about the position that will help you if you were to find your dream job one day. Tell them how these things are relevant to what you want to do someday.

Don't worry about admitting that you may someday move on, whether to join a different company or begin your own business. Employers don't expect anybody to work for them forever.

- Why are you leaving your current job?

This question could be a deal breaker.

Let's begin with things you shouldn't say. NEVER talk about how difficult your boss is. NEVER talk about not getting along with others. NEVER talk bad about the company. NEVER mention that your role or compensation is below your standards.

There might be legitimate reasons for leaving a job:

1. The current employer might not be able to give you any professional growth.

2. The current employer or department might be unstable.

Find a reason that the interviewer can't be worried about.

Try to focus on all the positive things a change of employers would bring. Tell them about what you would like to achieve. Tell them what you want to learn. Tell them about how you want to grow and the things you want to accomplish. Tell them how a move will be great for you and the company.

If you have a problem that concerns you that might be a deal breaker, by all means, mention it. Be prepared for them to take it one way or another. You might only want to work for a company that buys from vendors within a specific company. The interviewer will tell you if their company does this. If not, the interview will probably be over.

When you complain about your current employer, you are entertaining gossip. If you speak badly about one employer, you will do it with another.

- What work environment works best for you?

You might like working alone, but if you are interviewing for a job in a call center, using this answer is bad.

Take some time and think about the job you are interviewing for along with the culture of the company. If you like a flexible schedule, but the company doesn't have one, focus on another place. If you like to have support and direction, but the company wants its employees to be able to self manage, find another place.

Try to find ways the company will work for you. If you cannot find these, don't take the job. You will be miserable every single day.

- Why did you leave your last job?

This one is a bit tough. You shouldn't quit one job until you have another. However, life doesn't always work out this way. Did you leave because you didn't have enough time to look for your next job? Or because the company you were working for was closing, and you decided not to waste time waiting for them to shut the doors?

Many reasons are considered a necessity:

1. Harsh working conditions

2. Had to move to a new location for whatever reason

3. Health or family reasons

The only way to answer this question is to keep the answer short. Never try to expand your answer or include details.

- What was the hardest decision you've had to make in the past six months?

This question's goal is to see how well the person's reasoning ability, willingness to take risks, judgment, and problem-solving skills are.

Not having an answer would be a warning sign for a potential employer. Everybody makes hard decisions, no matter their position.

A good answer would prove that you can make hard reasoning based on an analytical decision. For example, would you be willing to wade through reams of data to figure out the best solution for the problem?

A great answer would prove you can make hard interpersonal decisions or hard data-driven decisions that might include interpersonal ramifications and considerations. Being able to make decisions that are based on data is helpful since almost all decisions will have an impact on most people. The best candidates will weigh up all sides of a problem, not just the human or business side.

- Why did you get fired?

This is a dangerous zone. This isn't the time to defend yourself with a sob story about being a victim.

If you made a mistake, you have to minimize how severe the situation was. Some might describe arguing with a boss as a difference of opinion. If your moral compass told you not to follow orders, this could be considered as "taking the high road".

NEVER cast the blame on other people. Think about finding a silver lining. Did you learn from the experience and thus now have some knowledge that will lessen the chances of it ever happening again?

Being laid off is not the same as being fired. If you were part of a huge company lay off, this is entirely different from being fired. It was a financial decision made by management, as you were in the group that was part of the budget cuts. Layoffs aren't usually personal; they are just business. People who hire staff know this, and have been involved in one at some point in their lives.

- Do you have a leadership style?

This is a rather hard question to answer without using a bunch of old clichés. Try to share leadership examples like, "The best way for me to answer that is to give you some examples of leadership challenges that I have faced," then share some situations where you handle the problem, worked through a crisis or motivated a team. Tell them what you did, and this will give the hiring manager a sense of how you will lead. It also lets you highlight some of your successes.

- Can you explain this gap in employment?

The main thing you need to do here is to make sure you give them a picture of you consistently doing something constructive, helping family, improving yourself, or being productive.

Interviewers don't want to hear that you needed a break from the rat race or you needed to recharge. The first thing that will pop into their minds is: When will you need another break? Will it be in the middle of that big project we have coming up?

- Have you ever disagreed with a manager's decision? How did you handle it?

Nobody will agree with all the decisions. Having disagreements is fine; it's what you do about the conflict that matters. We all know someone who loves to have a meeting after the meeting where they have supported a decision but then try to undermine it after the decision was made.

Show the interviewer you are a professional. Show them you voiced your concerns productively. If you can give them an example that will prove you can create change, wonderful. If not, show them that you support decisions even if you think they are wrong, as long as it isn't immoral or unethical.

Each company wants its employees to be forthright and honest, to share their concerns and issues, but to get behind decisions and support the company just like they agreed, even though they didn't.

- How would others describe you?

This is an awful question, but some interviewers might ask it. Here is a good answer: "I think people would say that what you see is what you get. If I say I am going to do something, I will do it. If I tell you I am going to help, I'll help. I'm not sure that everybody likes me, but they all know they can count on what I say and how hard I work."

- What was your salary in your last job?

This is another hard one. You need to be honest and open, but some companies will ask this question to begin salary negotiations.

Use an approach that skirts around the real issue but still gives them an answer. When they ask, reply with, "I'm focusing on jobs in the $50K range. Does this position pay in that range?" You should already know this, but it is a great way to deflect the question.

The interviewer might ask or they might not. If they press you for a definite answer, you will need to decide for yourself whether or not you want to share. Your answer isn't going to matter all that much since you will either accept the offered salary or not. It all depends on what you think is fair.

- What will we see you do in your first three months with us?

This answer should come from the employer. They should have expectations and plans laid out for you.

If you are asked, you can use the following as a guideline:

1. You will make a difference in bringing teamwork, a sense of commitment, focus, and enthusiasm to other employees and customers.

2. You will work hard to figure out how your job makes value. You won't just keep busy; you will keep busy doing the correct things.

3. You will stay focused on doing the things you do best. You will be hired since you bring specific skills and use these skills to make things happen.

4. You will learn how to help everyone around you: vendors, suppliers, customers, peers, employees, and the boss.

Now all you have to do is put in all the specifics that apply to the job and you.

- There is a snail inside a 30-foot well. Every day he can climb three feet, but each night he slides back down two. How long is it going to take him to get out of the well?

This type of question has become popular thanks to Google. The person doing the interview isn't looking for the correct answer so much as seeing how well you can reason.

The best thing to do if you aren't a math genius is to talk through the problem out loud while you are trying to solve the problem. Never be afraid to laugh at yourself if you get it wrong. At times they are trying to assess how well you deal with failure.

- What do you do when you aren't at work?

Most companies feel that a cultural fit is essential for their company. They take their employees outside interests as a way to figure out if you will fit well with the team they have already established.

Never let yourself be tempted into lying and telling them you like doing things you don't. Focus on hobbies or activities that show growth, such as goals you are working toward or skills you are learning. Put these into your details. Here is an example: "I am raising a family, so most of my time is focused on them, but I am using my commute time to learn Spanish."

- Do you have any questions for me?

You need to have questions. This is your time to interview the interviewer. This is your time to learn more about the company, its leadership style, its corporate culture, its role, and many other things you can think of.

People who are truly interested in the company will ask these questions. People who don't ask questions show they aren't truly interested but just trying to put feelers out to see how it "feels".

You need to know that the interview isn't over just because the interviewer asked this question. Good candidates use this as a time to shine.

You need to ask questions that do these things:

1. Show you have done your research about the company.

2. That will prompt a discussion or have interesting answers.

3. Mentions something else that is interesting and related to you.

Closing the Interview

You might not have a chance to address any shortcomings in an interview to follow up. You have to understand what was missing from the interview while you are still in the middle of the interview.

Once you have asked your questions, you want to confirm that you are the perfect candidate for the job. For you to do this, you have to probe the interviewer's mind and see if they still have concerns about you.

One final question to ask your interviewer is: "After discussing this job, I feel as if I would be a perfect fit for it. I'm curious to know if there is anything I said or DID NOT say that would make you believe otherwise."

Whatever answer you get to this question might open the door to something you weren't able to talk about during the interview or to clarify any misconceptions about something that was said.

Job Interview Checklist

The best way to make sure that you are confident in your interview is to be prepared. This will ensure that you make an amazing first impression and will help ease your nerves. The next time you have an interview, check off each of the following steps as you prepare. You do not have to do these things in the order that they are listed:

- *Get your clothes ready*

    o As you know, how you dress for an interview tells your potential employer a lot. The right outfit will let them know that you understand the company and its environment. This shows that you respect them.

- *Study the job listing*

    o Read back through the job advertisement and description to figure out exactly what the employer is looking for. Then, create a list of your personal and professional qualities, skills, and knowledge that fit into what they want. Make sure that you are ready to describe your attributes that show them you are the perfect fit.

- *Research the company*

  o This should fit right into the last step. Learn as much as you can about the company. This will also help you learn how you should dress for the interview as well. Look over their website, social media, and LinkedIn profiles of past and present employees. If you can, speak will some people who have worked for them. It also helps to get Google News to see if there has been any negative or positive press for them recently.

- *Contact company contacts*

  o To help boost your chances of getting hired, get a referral from a connection within the company. Having contacts who work for the company, or have worked for the company and left on good terms, can provide you with an inside track to getting hired. Potential employers like to interview people who come recommended. The contact can also let you know more about how the company's hiring process works.

- *Look over your resume*

  o If you have been asked for an interview, then they like what they saw on your resume. They are going to ask you about certain things on it, so make sure you are familiar with what it says. If you have a phone interview, you can have the resume in front of you, but you still shouldn't read directly off of it.

- *Come up with accomplishments that you can talk about*

o Hiring managers love to hear these things. These things should be on your resume, but either way, make sure that you have some facts and stories that you can share during the interview.

- *Find out who the interviewer is*

    o If at all possible, research some of the people that you will have to speak with. This will help you know how to prepare and say the right things to impress them.

- *Practice your interview questions*

    o Take some time to review some of the most common interview questions. This will give you a chance to frame your questions before you get surprised by them in the interview. This will help to reduce your stress. Get a family member or friend involved.

- *Be ready for questions about previous job changes*

    o The interviewer is likely going to ask you why you left your last job or why there is a gap in your employment. Make sure that you are ready to answer these questions. These things aren't bad, but what is bad is if you can't explain why.

- *Practice your technique*

    o What you say and how you act during an interview is either going to help or hinder you. While practicing your answers, practice how you sit, use your hands, and your eye contact.

- *Work on your etiquette*

    o Is bringing a cup of coffee or your cell phone okay? How should the interviewer be greeted? What do you need to bring with you? Make sure you brush up on the best interview etiquette so that you don't end up getting caught off guard.

- *Arrange transportation and get directions*

    o You have to know where you're supposed to go for your interview. Make sure you know exactly where to go and how long it will take you so that you aren't late or flustered. Check out the parking situation or public transport. You can also try a test run the day before to make sure that your directions are correct.

- *Have the right things with you*

    o You need to make sure that you know what to bring with you. You may need extra copies of your resume, reference list, a portfolio, and questions that you may have for them. Make sure you have everything ready to go. Pack them up the night before so that you don't forget them.

- *Send a quick thank you*

    o After you have had your interview, take the time to send the interviewer a thank you note. This helps to reinforce the fact that you are interested in the job. This is also a great time to address any concerns or issues that may have come up during the interview.

Conclusion

Thank for making it through to the end of *Job Interview: Will These Mistakes Cost You The Job?* It should have been informative and provided you with all of the tools you need to achieve your goals, whatever they may be.

Yes, job interviews are crazy and stressful, but with the right prep work, you can prove that you are worth a company's time and money. The next time you have an interview lined up, go through the checklist to make sure that you are prepared. The interview is the one thing standing between you and the job of your dreams, so don't let little mistakes prevent you from pursuing your dreams. Follow everything you have learned, and get any job that you want.

Finally, if you found this book useful in any way, a review on Amazon is always appreciated!